GW00359877

Meditations on Self-Discipline and Failure will make you pause and reflect, whether or not you agree with any or all of its contents. Written in the style of Marcus Aurelius' *Meditations*, and with a strong flavor of Epictetus, it confronts the reader with what happens if one looks at reality in the eyes and considers regulating his life accordingly. To do so takes both wisdom and courage, but Ferraiolo argues that it is well worth the effort.
Massimo Pigliucci, PhD, author of *How to Be a Stoic: Using Ancient Philosophy to Live a Modern Life*

Written in the spirit of Epictetus' *Manual*, Bill Ferraiolo's *Meditations* exposes the common human fallacies that lead to depression, anxiety, guilt, anger, and other toxic emotions. From the self-defeating desire to control the minds of others to the unrealistic demand that politicians tell the truth, Ferraiolo challenges the most insidious human tendencies to undermine one's own peace and solemnity. Read it, and always keep a copy close at hand.
Elliot D. Cohen, PhD, author of *What Would Aristotle Do? Self-Control through the Power of Reason*

Ferraiolo offers a provocative contemporary adaptation of his reading of the Stoic philosophers Marcus Aurelius and Epictetus and other ancient philosophers of similar minds. The book is well-organized and easy to read. It will be welcomed by anyone fascinated with or open to meditative philosophy of the Roman Stoic variety. An interesting and worthwhile read.
Hugh H. Benson, PhD, author of *Socratic Wisdom: The Model of Knowledge in Plato's Early Dialogues*

Meditations on Self-Discipline and Failure

Stoic Exercise for Mental Fitness

Meditations on Self-Discipline and Failure

Stoic Exercise for Mental Fitness

William Ferraiolo

BOOKS

Winchester, UK
Washington, USA

First published by O-Books, 2017
O-Books is an imprint of John Hunt Publishing Ltd., Laurel House, Station Approach,
Alresford, Hants, SO24 9JH, UK
office1@jhpbooks.net
www.johnhuntpublishing.com

For distributor details and how to order please visit the 'Ordering' section on our website.

Text copyright: William Ferraiolo 2016

ISBN: 978 1 78535 587 5
978 1 78535 588 2 (ebook)
Library of Congress Control Number: 2016951897

A CIP catalogue record for this book is available from the British Library.

Design: Stuart Davies

Printed and bound by CPI Group (UK) Ltd, Croydon, CR0 4YY, UK

We operate a distinctive and ethical publishing philosophy in all
areas of our business, from our global network of authors to
production and worldwide distribution.

CONTENTS

Dedication: For Jenny—my pebble

Acknowledgements

I would like to thank everyone at John Hunt Publishing for their assistance. Without Catherine Harris, Dominic C. James, Elizabeth Radley, John Hunt, Maria Barry, Mary Flatt, Nick Welch, Stuart Davies, and Krystina Kellingly, you would not have this book to read. Without the Roman Stoics, Socrates, and Diogenes, I would have had relatively little to write. Without my wife, Jennifer Ferraiolo, I would be no one.

Introduction

You are reading these words because you seek counsel and you have not quite found what you are looking for anywhere else. Had you found what you needed elsewhere, there would be no reason for you to continue searching, and no reason to look *here*, in particular. This seems a reasonable inference, does it not? It is entirely possible that you do not really know just what form of guidance you are seeking, or what exactly motivates you to wonder if you might be in need of any special assistance at all. In other words, you may not know what the problem is. Perhaps you have some idea of what the difficulty might be, but you struggle to articulate the problem clearly, or to explain it to anyone (including yourself) in a way that does not make it seem petty, or insignificant, or just another one of those common struggles that everyone has to face at some point or other. You do not want to be merely another whining, self-absorbed weakling who cannot handle daily life without running to Mommy, or some phony academic with a fancy degree or a television show — or call a psychic hotline! Life is hard. You get it. There is, however, something about your way of being in the world that is not quite comfortable. This is not a matter of body aches, bad furniture, or an air conditioner on the fritz. The discomfort that led you here is somewhere within the confines of your own consciousness. There is no salve for it. Ibuprofen does not help. It is not the kind of discomfort that can be rectified with more money, a bigger house in a better neighborhood, or even a dramatic change of location. Your career, or lack thereof, does not seem to be the source of the problem — although dissatisfaction in that area of your life might be a *symptom* of this condition that troubles you. Perhaps your relationships are less satisfying, or less comforting than you might have expected — but is that a *cause* of your discomfort, or is it an *effect*? Have people always experienced what you are going through now, or is it a feature of the "modern" world, and the constant hurrying, or the impersonal experiences of dealing with computers, recorded messages, and the greater isolation we seem to experience, paradoxically, as the population grows and becomes more dense—yet more distant, somehow? Maybe this is just some kind of phase you are going through, or a midlife crisis of some type, or an adolescent fixation on "finding yourself." Maybe your diet is out of whack. All that processed food, and microwaveable junk cannot be good for you, can it? Have you been watching too much television? Are you really getting the kind of restorative sleep that you need while tossing and turning on that mattress of yours? You know a lot of people who are taking antidepressants and antianxiety medications these days. There really is no shame in going to see a psychiatrist anymore, is there? Everybody seems to be doing it. Of course, not everybody seems to be getting much benefit out of it. The psychiatrists are doing pretty well for themselves, but their patients seem about as fouled up *after* "getting help" as they were before. Besides, how can you possibly know what kind of doctor or therapist you really need? Do you need to talk through your early childhood experience with some Freudian, or would you be better off with some hardcore cognitive-behavioral therapy, and bottle of Xanax to get you through those particularly rough patches at work, or on airplanes, or when your mother-in-law comes to visit? If you could just find something to help you deal with your stress, and a way of calming yourself down when it all gets to be just a little too much, then you could handle the rest on your own. Of course, you are not quite certain what "it" is, or why "it" gets to be "too much" so often that you find yourself reading this, and thinking about drugs and headshrinkers. What are you unable to "handle" exactly, and what does it even mean to "handle" your life? Life is for living! When did "handling" your life become a legitimate goal? Your mother probably has something to do with this. Shrinks *always* blame the mother—because she always causes the problem! Who was your earliest influence? Who taught you your first lessons? Whose belly did you live in for nine months? You could call Mom, if she is still available, and talk it over. Of course, that would just be a nightmare! Criticism is bound to fly back and forth. You will end up feeling guilty—which is not particularly helpful. Mom will stop talking to you—for a while. No, you need something else. You need to figure this out for *yourself*.

Luckily, you are reading just the right book. There is no complex theory presented here for you to absorb, ponder, and then try to apply to your own life in some step-by-step fashion. You will find no twelve step program explained in these pages, and you will not be encouraged to join any organization, or club, or religious cult, or any other outfit that charges dues and issues newsletters. You will find no case studies here. You will not be instructed to confess to anything, issue apologies to anyone, or attend any seminar. You will find *one* thing in this book. You will read *meditations*. This is not meditating in the style of Eastern wisdom traditions like Buddhism or Hinduism (although there is nothing wrong with those practices). These are meditations as we find them in a lot of Western philosophy and religion. You will not, however, need to know much about those academic areas (although there is nothing wrong with learning some of that stuff). No, you just read along and, maybe every once in a while, stop to consider whether what you are reading applies to your life and your struggles. You will find that a lot of it does.

As you may have noticed by now, this book is written in the second person—which just means that the word "you" desig-nates the meditator. Of course, you (reader) did not *write* these meditations, but that does not prevent you from thinking your own thoughts about what you find here. In fact, *nothing* prevents you from thinking your own thoughts—ever! You may identify that running theme as you read along. Think for *yourself*. The words you read may prompt you to reconsider some things, or to consider some other things for the first time, and you may have a very different experience than another reader of the same text— but that really is part of the point. Each reader adds a different set of experiences to the writing. The Roman Emperor, Marcus Aurelius, wrote his meditations in a book that he kept with him over a period of years, and he would return to these collected thoughts every so often to remind himself of what he really valued, what kind of person he intended to be, and what sort of life he thought was worth living. The book he wrote was originally entitled *To Himself*, and he may have intended it only for his own use. After his death, however, someone found it, published it with the title, *Meditations*, and people have been reading it ever since. It has been a great source of comfort for about two thousand years. Marcus Aurelius was an actual *philosopher king*. The ancient Greek philosopher Plato had hoped that there would be a real one someday. He wrote a few things about philosophers becoming kings, or kings learning philosophy. Some of it is even worth reading. For your purposes, however, you will not need to know much of anything about Plato, Marcus Aurelius, or any of the other handful of historical figures that are mentioned in a few places in this book. They are just examples of people who tried very hard to figure out some of the same things that you are trying to figure out. Some were pretty admirable characters. If you have never heard of this one or that one, there is no need to worry. The point of the meditation in question never depends upon you knowing who Diogenes was, or what Epictetus said and did, or anything like that. The first guy was an ancient Cynic philosopher, and the second guy was a Stoic. You do not need to know what any of that means (although there is nothing wrong with finding out if you feel like it). Just read and let yourself think about what "you" seem to be dealing with.

The deepest struggles that we all face, the difficulties that keep us up at night, and the concerns that cause us to wonder if we are living the lives that we ought to be living cannot always be addressed in language suited to a seventh-grade reading level. The words get a little "fancy" now and again. This is *not* for show. The deepest recesses of your mind, where the greatest discomfort arises and festers, is just not the kind of subject area that can be explained to the average twelve-year-old. Are *you* an average twelve-year-old? If so, you may want to leave this book on the shelf for a few more years. If not, then you may want to read on. It is not an *easy* read, but nothing worthwhile is ever all *that* easy. It is also not a particularly *pleasant* read. The word "Failure" appears in the title, after all. Also, "Self-Discipline" is generally kind of difficult to master. Ask a Marine or a Navy Seal. You will find a *lot* of self-criticism here, and a lot of discussion of unpleasant experiences. Do not be frightened by the unpleasantness, and try not to take the criticism personally. Remember, *you* did not write this stuff. The author did that, and the author's mental life is, frankly, not *yours*—and you need not trouble yourself about the contents of someone else's mind. That is another running theme you may notice. *You*, however, and *your* thoughts, and *your* character, and *your* behavior, *are* your business. Ultimately, they are the *only* things that are really up to you. *That* is what these meditations are all about. What do you, and you *alone*, control? What kind of person do *you* want to be? Get started *becoming* what you want to be. You never know how much time is left. Turn your attention *inside*. The truth is there. You just have to be willing to look for it. Good luck.

Book I

1

You can control nothing other than your own attitudes, values, and efforts directed at mental discipline. The rest of the world is as it is, will be as it will be, and unfolds as it does with or without your consent. This is as it should be. Indeed, this is as it *must* be. You have enough to contend with just governing your own thoughts and actions. Your consciousness and your will are more than enough to keep you busy, engaged, and challenged. Master yourself, administer your affairs, discipline yourself, and you will have accomplished more than most ever dare. This is your only purpose. Are you not ashamed to allow the events of the day to throw you off balance? What business is it of yours if lives begin or end, warfare erupts here or peace is restored there, economies shudder, earthquakes strike, or storms beat down upon the land? Will it all to be otherwise if you can. What answers directly to the exertion of your will? That, and *only* that, is your business. Do not invite needless distress and perturbation by insisting that the world must conform to your expectations or whims. Who, after all, do you think you are? Control the very small sphere that answers to your direction. As for the rest, cultivate gratitude for the opportunity to draw breath and take part in a life that you never earned.

2

Other people are not yours to control. You may speak to them, cajole them, debate them, show them evidence, present them with the dictates of reason, you may even threaten them—but their minds are their own. You invite needless frustration, anger, animosity, and discontent every time you insist that they must agree with you, or respect you, or love you, or adopt any particular cast of mind. Their will is beyond your direct control.

Make your best efforts to assist them, if it seems reasonable to do so, but do not allow your contentment to depend upon anyone else's mental state or other measurement of well-being. The world will have its way with all of us. The story of every human life ends in that human's death. To resist or resent this is childish folly. To insist that those whom you love must be invulnerable to suffering, struggle, and death, is to insist that mortal and fragile humanity is insufficient for the maintenance of your contentment. Is the human condition displeasing to you? Perhaps you ought to register a complaint with management and insist upon some type of compensation. Then again, perhaps you would do better to grow up, stop your whimpering, and try not to be a malignancy upon this world that has no need of you.

3

You need not take seriously anyone's alleged "right" not to be "offended" (whatever that supposedly means). Another person's mental states are entirely beyond your control and ought, therefore, to lie entirely beyond your concern as well. Why should you care what anyone else thinks, or allow yourself to be troubled by what anyone else says? Just as your thoughts are up to you, so are theirs up to them. Let others govern the speech that comes out of their mouths, and take no heed of it—even if it is directed at you or is allegedly about you. If what they say is true, learn from it. If what they say is untrue, then their false descriptions are no business of yours. Should someone else believe a false characterization of you, someone thereby develops a misperception. What of it? They are free to believe as they will, and their mistakes need not concern you. No one can make a misperception true or accurate. Concern yourself only with the truth. What others *believe* the truth to be is *their* concern.

4

Success and failure do not, in any way, depend upon states of affairs that lie beyond the direct control of your will. Your performance is largely up to you (providing that your body does not fail your will). Another person's assessment of your performance is entirely beyond your control. You must, therefore, jettison any concern regarding someone else's assessment of your performance. This applies to your career, your relationships, and the improvement of your character. Do everything in your power to be a virtuous person, a good human being, a proper spouse and parent, and a useful professional. If you do as well as you are able in these endeavors, you need not concern yourself about whether anyone believes that you have done well or not. Do not lie. Tell the truth, and do not concern yourself with anyone who says that you lie. Do not commit adultery. Ignore those who accuse you of committing adultery. Be conscientious about your work. Do not concern yourself with those who question your diligence. Be a good person. Be an honorable person. That is enough.

5

Resist being swayed by the opinions of the majority or those who regard themselves as your peers. Opinions are insignificant, ephemeral things. Opinions occupying the minds of others are even less significant than your own. Concern yourself only with evidence and reason. If your opinion does not comport with the available evidence, relinquish it. Do not take it up again unless you encounter new evidence supporting it. Resist the urge to agree simply for the sake of seeming agreeable. Resist the urge to consent for the sake of conviviality. You have no obligation to comport felicitously with the poorly informed, the disingenuous, or the dim. Let them think what they will of you, and remain indifferent to the contempt with which they regard you. Their beliefs are none of your concern. Focus on understanding the world around you, your place in it, and your duties as a rational and decent human being. The rest is theater. Leave it to the actors.

6

Do not pretend to respect other persons either more or less than you actually do respect them. You owe no one a pretense of deference, and you owe everyone the deference that they have, by your own lights, earned. You should have nothing to do with sham collegiality or faux civility. Some persons are worthy of your contempt, and their behavior, as well as other outward indications of their character, is sufficient grounds for reasonable (though not perfectly reliable) assessment of their merit. If anyone demands that you "try to get along" with any person that you do not respect, then you have grounds for reconsidering your relations with the former individual (the one issuing the demand). Do not allow yourself to be pressed, bullied, or cajoled into relations that strike you as unhealthy or pointless.

7

Inevitability is double-edged sword. You may perceive that a particular change is both inevitable and not at all worthy of celebration. Indeed, the inevitable can be, and often is, quite repugnant. Faced with an unpleasant inevitability, you would do well to reconcile yourself to it, and reject despair, anger, and frustration concerning the matter. This is not tantamount to surrender. The inevitable is not necessarily bound to be permanent or even particularly long-lived. That too shall pass away. Endure it as best you can. Keep searching for an opportunity to make some change should the chance to do so arise. Do not *insist* upon this chance arising. Do not peg your contentment to this opportunity, but prepare yourself so that you can respond rationally if events offer you an opening. There is no excuse for failing to prepare for what you see coming. There is no excuse for allowing a valuable opportunity to pass, while you stand dumbly by. Perceive. Reason. Act.

8

You see your nation and its culture in precipitous decline. Both appear to be moribund and well beyond salvation. Certainly, both are well beyond the sphere of *your* direct control. Your will is impotent beyond the direction of your thoughts, your actions, and your decisions. What then will you do with *your* life, and *your* share of allotted time? Remember that you do not know how much that share will turn out to be. You also have no idea how long your nation, or Western culture at large, are likely to endure. These are "yours" only in the sense that you were born into them. They are not yours to control. You had no hand in creating either. Do not cling to a dying enterprise. Be prepared to jump before the vehicle goes over the cliff.

9

There appears to be relatively little time left. The time for what you had previously held dear has almost certainly elapsed. Your only rational option then is to alter your concerns, and to direct your attention *inside*. That which is beyond your will must be allowed to slip beyond your concern. It should not recede from your *notice*, but you must not tether your peace of mind to it. The world will have its way. The world, indeed, *must* have its way. It is not your place to grumble against the course of events. It is not your place to grumble at all. Adapt or take your place in the implosion.

10

To love others is noble, but to despair at their mortality and fragility is nothing but an invitation to needless suffering and impotent anxiety. Do not become overly hard-hearted, but do not deny your limitations with respect to your ability to secure the well-being of your loved ones. The world is brutal and pitiless. Do not insist upon the contrary. Everyone about whom you have ever cared is going to die. Some have passed on already. In fact, *everyone,* irrespective of any connection to you (or lack thereof), is bound to go "the way of all flesh." Do not wish it to be otherwise. This is petulant childishness. Embrace mortality. What, after all, is the alternative?

Book II

1

Pity and sentimentality are of little if any use to you or to others. Surely, little is accomplished by commiseration among those beset by despair. Indeed, despair itself is of little value unless it prompts one to shed it and move forward in noble and rational fashion. Every moment of self-pity is a moment of diminution, a moment wasted, a moment spent in shame. Feeling sorry for yourself is a manifestation of irrationality and weakness. The world exists, you have an opportunity to draw breath and participate, and you *dare* to indulge in self-pity? If the challenge is too great, take to the exit! Otherwise, steel yourself and get to work. It is not your proper role to whimper. Leave that to the mongrels.

2

Do events disappoint you? If so, do you, therefore, blame the events? This is foolishness. Events unfold as they will, or as someone or something far more powerful than you directs them to unfold. Do not set yourself up as an adversary opposing the world, its evolution, or the passing scene. This is a futile and childish opposition. Your business is the governance of yourself and your will. The rest is, to be blunt, none of your business. The time is now. Help is *not* on the way. Here is the world as it is. Here you are. What do you intend to do about it? If you feel the slightest uncertainty about the matter, you have a *lot* of work to do.

3

Be mindful of the lessons you learn, and of the sources from which you learn them. Beware the tendency to focus on short-term benefits. Never sacrifice your integrity for any form of material gain. Do not degrade yourself. Remember also that no one else has the power to degrade you. More importantly (perhaps), beware the temptation to degrade yourself through the pursuit of ignoble goals, or the satisfaction of bestial impulses, at the expense of misused reason, atrophied virtue, and indifference to honor and decency. If you overvalue the lesser, you have learned nothing from the examples of Socrates, Epictetus, and Diogenes. This is worse than a shame.

4

No one is master of his own fate. No one is master of any domain beyond his own will and its sphere of direct influence. You possess the wherewithal, however, to increase mastery of *yourself*. Bend your will to *that* purpose. Focus your efforts on matters that respond to the exertion of your will. Do not attempt to change the weather. Adapt to its changes, and do not complain of heat, rain, or snow. This is not your business. Can you master your own mind? Can you learn to govern yourself in admirable fashion? Can you face any contingency with a full heart and steady hands? Let fate hurl at you what it will. Something, at some point, will break. Take care that it is not *you*.

5

Your detractors provide valuable lessons. Ask yourself if their criticisms are correct. If so, then improve yourself, and be grateful for their guidance. If, on the other hand, their criticisms are misguided, then recognize that their error is nothing to you. Let them persist in their misperceptions if they must. Should they change their minds and come to respect you, recognize that this is equally insignificant. Perhaps the praise will prove as well or ill-placed as the criticism. Perhaps both assessments will prove inapt and inaccurate. What of it? The wind blows, the people form beliefs, the river flows, and, in the end, the world swallows it all.

6

Kindness toward animals is an almost unalloyed good. It is soothing for you, it is pleasurable for the animal, and it is reassuring to those who may witness the kindness. You must, however, take care that you correctly distinguish the tame animal from that one that despises the touch of humankind. The latter is not likely to return your affection. You need not pet every snake and porcupine you encounter. A skunk is not entitled to an embrace, and a lion has no desire to sit content in your lap. Kindness within reason is a virtue. Pathological, indiscriminate kindness is a recipe for personal disaster and cultural extinction. Do not gleefully participate in your own destruction.

7

Do not make excuses. This is an ignoble habit, and you diminish yourself with each new excuse you offer. Even a "good" excuse, even offered in sincerity, contributes to the decline of your character. Bear the consequences of your actions, and the disapprobation that generally ensues, in the manner of a rational adult in possession of your faculties. Embrace the fair and the unfair criticisms alike. Do not complain about either. A complaint is indistinguishable, in the only analysis that matters, from a dog's bark, or the bleating of the sheep. Making an unpleasant sound with your face is hardly a method of ennobling your soul or your character. Can you manage no better?

8

You will encounter stupidity, lies, and corruption every day of your life. It is your obligation to do everything in your power to ensure that these do not originate with you. Secondarily, you must resist the temptation to become frustrated with the stupid, the liars, and the corrupt. This is, perhaps, your greatest challenge. Let them degrade themselves, but do not degrade yourself because of them. Their character *is* their punishment. It is not your concern. It is not your role to attempt to rectify another person's character. Do you not perceive enough of your *own* flaws, regarding which you would do far better by applying your attention and your efforts? Until you become an honorable, virtuous, and wise human being, you are excused from responsibility for setting the world aright, and perfecting the unwashed masses. Arrogance is unbecoming. Unwarranted arrogance is a grotesque disfigurement.

9

Politicians are, by and large, not to be trusted. Are the citizens, or the voters, any worthier of trust than their "representatives"? You have spent too many years living among your fellow human beings to take their indignation, feigned or forthright, more seriously than a politician's promises. Would *you* be more honest, more upright, or more admirable sitting in some seat of power than is its current occupant? Do not be as naïve as that. You have never had the opportunity to wield that type of power, you have no way of knowing how doing so would impact your behavior or your character, and all available evidence suggests that the citizenry would be no better off with you in a governing role. Have you even learned to govern *yourself* in virtuous fashion? Rather than casting a critical eye upon Governors, Senators, Presidents, and the like, you would be well served to turn your gaze inward. Do you not perceive corruption within yourself? Are you not one of the citizens "represented" by the corrupt politicians? How unlucky you must be to have been hurled into this wicked old world, with such a pristine heart, mind, and soul! Do not deceive yourself in this manner. Do not be a child.

10

People have lived through far more difficult and challenging times than those confronting you—and the best among them remained persons of virtue and courage. What excuse do you manufacture for faltering where they did not? If you are a lesser being, then your failure is as it should be. Certainly, a deficient soul cannot complain of trying times. If you are not a lesser being, then set about becoming what you are capable of being, and do not poison the world with whining about circumstance. There is no need of another simpering weakling on the surface of the planet. Can you not face the world as it is? Must it be softened for you? It is best not to hold your breath waiting for the requisite adjustments to assuage your concerns. Then again, if the alternative is griping about an "unfair" world, and "unjust" company, perhaps holding your breath, as well as your tongue, would be something of an improvement. Better this than continuing to stamp your feet and gripe like a peevish child.

Book III

1

All politics is largely theater. It is a Kabuki dance, and those engaged in the dance wear masks or painted faces. They are personae—not persons. Are you enraged by their corruption and dissimulation? If so, you hope for more from them than is reasonable. Do not expect swarming vipers to weave a tapestry honoring truth, justice, and virtue. You are old enough, you have lived long enough, and you have seen and heard enough to know better. Did the Athenians not execute Socrates? Was Julius Caesar not assassinated by his best friend? Have you not read Machiavelli's *The Prince*? Did Plato not extol the necessity of "The Noble Lie"? Did your parents not tell you the stories of Santa Claus, the Easter Bunny, and the Tooth Fairy? Now, you allow yourself to be shocked, disappointed, and disenchanted with corrupt, lying politicians? For God's sake, stop telling yourself that the world "ought to be" filled with honest, wholesome folk. Why "ought" it to be so, and why "ought" these honest, wholesome folk rise to positions of political power? Backstabbing and deceit have been staples of the political arena since the days before history began to be recorded. Your disillusionment is entirely your own doing.

2

The length of your life is not nearly as important as the quality of the person living it. Far better for you that you should live a shorter, but nobler life, than that you should continue in malingering mediocrity. A time is likely to come for asking yourself what your life was ultimately about. It is better to have an answer than a shrug. Do you wish to be like a bridge that spans the river, but collapses under the weight of the smallest vehicle? Live one day in nobility, and you will have accomplished more than ten thousand lives of desperate, quarrelsome, hapless commoners. Perhaps they can have managed no better. Perhaps the same is true of you and your inveterate weakness. What, after all, commends the life that you have lived up to this point? What, if anything, sets you apart from the common folk? Be careful that you do not catch yourself looking down your nose at those with whom you are, in fact, eye level.

3

There is a time for violence. Do not delude yourself with sentimentality about this matter. Perhaps this is as it must be, perhaps not—perhaps there is no such thing as what "should be." None of that is up to you. The decision to engage in violence, to use it as a tool for some noble purpose is, however, yours to make. Also, you must distinguish the noble purpose from the base satisfaction of mere urge or impulse. Should the need arise, the failure to resort to the requisite ferocity is nothing short of cowardice. Do not tell yourself that it is mere indifference that stays your hand, or that it is disdain or contempt that forestalls your engagement. If you are responsible for the defense of yourself, your family, your community, or the innocent, and if you fail to act at the crucial moment, then you will know that you are a useless, pusillanimous weakling. Should you also deceive yourself about your failure, you are a lesser being still.

4

The body ages. The body fails. The body responds only very imperfectly to the commands of your will. As long as you possess a tool, however, it is wise to keep it in reasonably good repair. Learn the fundamentals, at least, of basic body mechanics, nutrition, and general "maintenance." Little that is good or worthwhile arises from wasted potential. Your body is not *you*, but it is not *nothing* either. How many times have you disparaged, at least in your own mind, those who have "let themselves go," or those who seem never to have troubled themselves about physical conditioning? You are not permitted to fall into hypocrisy on this front. Do not allow your muscles to atrophy, or your belly to become an encumbrance. Test your reflexes and hand-eye coordination on a regular basis. Practice functional conditioning, and not mere body building for aesthetic purposes. Should the need arise, your body, mind, and character must all rise to the occasion as one cohesive enterprise. A body that cannot obey the dictates of the will is nothing more than a corpse that has not yet expired.

5

A degree of skepticism is healthy. Indeed, life is probably unlivable in a condition of complete credulity. You must do your best to distinguish between beliefs supported by evidence, and those that are based entirely, or largely, upon wishful thinking. *Radical* skepticism is, however, not particularly useful. Was Pyrrho of Elis an admirable spirit, or was he merely a contrarian, determined to confound the philosophers of his day? Is it possible to be both of these? Surely, there have always been "wise men" in need of humbling. In any event, some "faith," in some degree, is almost certainly indispensable to an active life, and to active engagement with the world and oneself. Your beliefs must rest upon *some* foundation lying beneath any practicable scrutiny. Otherwise, doubt is likely to paralyze and stultify your efforts. Move forward with a willingness to question yourself, and without reluctance to face questioning by others—but move forward nonetheless.

6

The impulse to be disgusted by popular culture is, all too frequently, verging upon the irresistible. Often, it seems a weakness to experience anything less than revulsion at the sad, pathetic spectacle unfolding all around you. Tempting though it may be, you are not excused from your responsibility to maintain a rational, but informed, disinterest regarding celebrities, notables, politicians, and their many follies. Repudiation without understanding is not a virtuous disposition of character. Sincere repudiation requires sufficient comprehension of that which you repudiate to provide justification should your opposition face challenge or scrutiny. Merely saying, "I will take no part in this," without the capacity to explain *why* you decline to participate, constitutes nothing more than a retreat before an enemy you fear to know.

7

Weakness is *never* virtue. In some cases it is vice. In others, it is simple dysfunction or incapacity. Do not allow yourself to be drawn into it. Do not permit weakness to become a reflexive state of your character. It beckons to the *worst* in you. There seems to be little hope that you can purge weakness altogether. You are, after all, one product of millions of years of evolution, and the fight or flight instinct includes that second option for good reason. There are dangers from which flight is the only alternative to destruction. You should not, however, allow flight to become your default response to all dangers, all challenges, and all bogeymen (real or imagined) that may arise. The world is, indeed, fraught with peril. The real danger, the one with which you are to be most acutely concerned, is the danger of becoming a coward and a weakling. The world can (and will) kill you, break your body, and deprive you of material possessions, but only *you* can deprive yourself of dignity and honor.

8

Nietzsche extolled the virtues of the "Superman." What objection arises from any source other than weakness, any intuition apart from the perspective of the sheep, any worldview that is not obstructed by the shuffling, grunting, bleating herd? Genius is entitled to recognition and reverence. Isaac Newton was not merely another scientist. Alexander was far more than just another warrior. Michelangelo was no dunce with the brush and the chisel. Only at the peril of your own character and your own "soul" (for lack of a better term) do you avert your eyes from greatness, and from the men who impose their will upon the world around them. The sheep will always resent the wolf. The wolf devours the sheep—and suffers no pangs of conscience for it. Is there more of the prowling wolf in you, or are you more cowering sheep than you care to admit? Do you tend to identify with predator, or with prey? Perhaps you seek some third option. Is this not, itself, a telling inclination? The predator does not seek to remove itself from the hunt and the kill. Without these, its purpose goes unfulfilled. What are *you* lacking that deprives you of fulfillment? You have not tasted blood for some time now.

9

Do not allow yourself to begin desiring those things that are common desiderata among the masses, or those things that advertisers tell you that you "need." Your true needs are few, and most of them are fairly readily satisfied. Do not bankrupt yourself or your family chasing artificial "necessities," or trivial material possessions. Concern with greater material wealth than is required can only induce anxiety, and instigate envy, or other ignoble states of mind. Do not cheapen yourself with obsession about money. Though it is often misquoted and misunderstood, scripture tells us that the *love* of money is the root of all evil, and a trap the virtuous must avoid. Wealth does not deserve adoration. The pecuniary impulse is bound to engender pettiness of spirit, and malevolence in pursuit of ever more control over the material world. None of that constitutes a proper object of your affection. Is it not, at root, love of *self* that inspires evil? Remember that *you* are no more a proper object of your affection than is anything that money can buy.

10

Distinguish carefully between persons or virtuous character and those who merely pretend to value decency. The world swarms with the latter, whereas the former are treasures that amply reward those who search diligently for them. As for the pretenders, you need not deprive them of their cherished illusions. Perhaps they sleep better at night believing that their neighbors, if not themselves, think them admirable. It is not necessary to expose every fraud, or reveal every poseur—nor is there sufficient time or manpower for the task. Leave them be. Thus, you will free yourself to spend time associating with persons of genuine virtue and authentic honor. Find them where you can. Follow them where they go. Absorb as many lessons as possible from conversation, observation, and let their excellence "rub off on you" if any of it can be attained in that manner. The company you keep tells at least as much of the story of your character as does the saga of your deeds and dreams. Do not declare your love of virtue, principle, and honor while sharing fellowship with charlatans and miscreants.

Book IV

1

Do not become overly enamored with yourself, your abilities, or your paltry status. You are, in the grand scheme of things, a trifling, ephemeral phenomenon of little consequence. You are slightly smarter than an ape or a dolphin. If there is a Creator who has endowed you with any special status, recognize that this is a *gift* and *not* an *accomplishment* in which you may rightfully take pride. No one *earns* birth as a member of the reasoning species, or any privileges pertaining thereto. If the matter is entirely propitious, you have still less warrant for a swollen ego. Note your good *fortune*, but do not claim to be *intrinsically good*, due to a chance concatenation of molecules. Set about the business of trying to understand your place in this vast cosmos, your duties as a human being, and a method and practice leading to enlightenment—or the closest approximation you can manage.

2

You perceive a collapse on the horizon. Neither you, nor anyone else, can predict precisely when it will take place, and the consequences are unknowable as well. Rome fell. You are in no position to insist upon a better or different fate for your society and your culture. It seems that certain elements of the culture decline first, and the rest ineluctably follows. Prepare. Do not allow your true self, your will and your character to "fall" as well. Master yourself, and your capacity to respond rationally when conditions beyond your control require both clear perception and a cool head. More than your own survival and well-being may hang in the balance. Those who depend upon you may be helpless without your counsel and guidance. Even if you cannot compel them to obey, you can, nonetheless, provide them direction and advice. When you are called upon to lead in an emergency, do not shy away from this responsibility. Do the best you are able to secure necessities to those for whom you are responsible. Beyond that, remember that events will unfold of their own accord, or at the command of powers beyond your control. Do not *resist*—adapt.

3

Practice gratitude. Remind yourself each day of your good fortune, and of the many unearned benefits you have enjoyed. Some may begrudge you these gifts of fortune. Let them do so. Spend neither time nor energy debating your detractors. What is their judgment to you? Your will has no purchase within the confines of their minds. Do not, therefore, venture into that arena. Do not even attempt to peer inside. Your own thoughts, attitudes, and behaviors are more than enough to occupy all of your efforts and concerns. Criticism cannot alter your character. It cannot turn you into something you are not, or compel you to adopt a persona that is disingenuous or artificial. Criticism is noise. Can noise dishonor you? Can it deprive you of your decency? Certainly not. Only you can diminish yourself in such ways. Your critics have their own problems. Leave them be.

4

Beware the tendency to identify too strongly with groups of people with whom you have only tenuous associations. Do not make an idol of your nation, your culture, your race, or your extended family. None of these are virtuous through-and-through or sufficiently pure to warrant worship. Keep this in mind when it comes to rooting for sports teams and the like. Is this a noble, honorable organization or institution? Why should a team, especially one of which you are not a member, winning or losing impact your frame of mind in any way? Is it not foolish to become angry or disappointed because of what a group of grown men or women do, or fail to do, with a ball? Let allegiances of this type drive others to distraction, if they are so inclined. Your only legitimate allegiance is to the pathway of wisdom, virtue, and the pursuit of truth. Find the team that treads this same path, and you will have found companions worthy of applause.

5

Your vices are your own. Do not blame nature, environment, or heredity for your failures. All of those lie beyond the influence of your will and your decisions. If nature has made you flawed, and it *has*, then your business is to make the best of your circumstances and improve yourself within nature's limitations. Do not moan about your inadequacies. Recognize them, distinguish between what you can and cannot do about these imperfections, and then exert effort only where it may do some good. The rest is simply *not* up to you. Your innate intellect is nothing special. So be it. What can you accomplish with the middling mind you have been granted? You are, physically, fairly run-of-the-mill. Shall you grieve that you were not born an Adonis or a Hercules? Where is the benefit in so doing? Improve your body as much as is necessary for the pursuit of your true purpose. You are not, after all, training for the Olympics. Take notice of those dealing with far greater dysfunctions in these areas, and be thankful for the poor endowments you have.

6

Recognize that the world will have its way. The world is neither your adversary not your ally. The world, in fact, takes no notice of you at all. It requires only that you die at some point. This is, really, not so much to ask. Who has yet failed to honor nature's measly request? When it is your time to die, try to make a dignified exit. There is no need for histrionics about the matter, and making a melodrama of your last days will do you no good in any event. The world will not stand still when you depart. Millions "shuffle off this mortal coil" every day, and you have only paused to note the passing of a handful. Is your demise, somehow, an event of greater moment than these others? Do not even waste time and effort considering such an absurd proposition. Some billions of years down the road, our sun will explode in a supernova, incinerating this entire planet and every trace of life that ever existed anywhere on its surface. Do you want your name chiseled on a building when the conflagration strikes? Fame, fortune, power, and all the rest of the human enterprise will, in the end, come to nothing. This is not punishment. This is not cruel fate. This is simply the way of things. It is neither wrong nor right. It is brute fact. What is your objection?

7

Who are you to complain about *anything*? Do you claim to have been mistreated? Do you claim to have suffered needlessly? Who has not suffered? Whose suffering was more or less "necessary" than the rest? How many have suffered *far* more than you? *Most* have, have they not? To weep and bemoan your fate is ingratitude, self-absorption, and weakness. You abase yourself with every gripe and alleged grievance. Your obligation is to improve yourself as best as you are able in the time you are allotted — and never forget that you know not how long it is. This is not accomplished by whining and hurling accusations. Get on with it! No one can possibly have abused, wronged, or victimized you a fraction as often as you have done these things to yourself. You waste your time and energy on nonsense. You degrade yourself with servility and supplication. You are granted human life, and you throw it away on grumbling and wishing for better. How dare you moan about your condition? A beast in a cage is not as querulous as you.

8

Do not toy with that which is forbidden. Do not feign ignorance regarding such matters, either. You may not *always* be certain about what is, and is not, permissible, but do not pretend a pervasive inability to discern virtue and distinguish it from vice. Guideposts are available. Do not ignore the counsel of sages or the timeless maxims of prudence and good judgment. Do not claim that you have not heard the inner voice of conscience. Others may speak in such ways, and perhaps some speak truly. It is neither safe nor wise to assume that everyone has access to the same sources of guidance, or the same proclivities concerning adherence to counsel. *You*, however, *have* been warned. You *have* been taught. You have had the advantage of wise counsel dropped more or less into your lap. You have been shown the way to wisdom and virtue. So, do as you have been told. Stay on the *narrow* path.

9

Failure, or what the world *calls* "failure," is not to be feared. There is neither shame nor derogation in it. The only real failure is insufficient self-discipline or inadequate effort aimed at self-improvement. Events beyond your control cannot constitute genuine failure, but only failure as it may be conceived in the minds of other persons. You lost a contest, failed an exam, or found yourself or your work rejected. Perhaps you were held up as an object of derision for it. What is that to you? Let them call you what they will, and say about you what they like. Their words are just sounds they make with their faces. Consider your own *internal* failures of will, if you find them. Look always to govern *yourself* as best you are able. Having done so, take no heed of your detractors. They are bound to be as their character dictates. To what end do you take their criticisms and disparagement to heart? Your business lies elsewhere. Turn your critical gaze *inside*, and determine whether any of the criticism has merit. If so, be grateful for the assistance and improve. If not, rational indifference to ridicule is called for. Mockery in no way devalues your honest effort. Laugh along. Enjoy the show.

10

Incompetence has become ubiquitous. Do not allow yourself to be surprised or frustrated by your encounters with it. If the incompetence is your own (and sometimes it *is*), work diligently to improve yourself, and make every possible effort to avoid similar failures in the future. If the ineptitude is not your own, but afflicts another, take note of the matter, but do not fret over the consequences or berate anyone. Observation and understanding are sufficient for your purposes—providing, of course, that they are associated with the fortitude to correct any inadequacy that lies within your power. The temptation to become enervated is bound to arise, but you must resist it with as much energy as you can muster. Lethargy is no answer to incompetence. You may have to redouble your efforts to compensate for some instance of stupidity or other. If so, then set about the redoubling. Has *your* stupidity never cost anyone else an added effort? Do not spend so much time in the remembrance of such cases that your life passes you by. Work harder. Do not complain. Be an adult.

Book V

1

Do not invest time and emotional energy imagining calamities that might befall you or your family and friends. Be aware of the possibilities, prepare as best as you are able to avoid needless suffering, loss of life, financial disaster, and the like and, certainly, learn how to respond rationally and efficiently should the need arise. Do not, however, obsess in macabre fashion, or succumb to despair over troubles merely conceived, or disasters not yet incurred. It is unwise to fret about the mere *chance* that things may go awry. This chance is ubiquitous and pervasive. Just about anything *could* go wrong. It is unwise and wasteful to conflate the merely possible with the probable—or the inevitable. Your role as protector and defender of the family is, as yet, unchallenged. Luckily, there has been very little in the way of resentment about your exercise of the relevant duties. Do not perseverate on dark or morbid curiosities. Your protective function is more felicitously served with clear eyes, and an agile mind, unencumbered with ghoulish fancy.

2

Be grateful for your family, and for your opportunities to learn what it means to be a virtuous member of a thriving clan. In serving them admirably, you improve yourself more than you improve their circumstances. Being good to them is one of the best ways to become a better servant of the public good, as well as a better human being. Your kinfolk are not to be treated as mere equals-among-others. They are, for you, very specific others, and your obligations toward them supersede those in nearly any other arena. While it is true that everyone is somebody's child, it is also true that *not* everyone is *your* child, or spouse, or parent, or sibling. Do not be taken in by specious arguments about equality or universality when it comes to unique duties based in biological, or otherwise intimate, associations. It is no vice to love "your own" in a manner that you do not offer to the rest of humanity. If you have the wherewithal to extend your affections further, without jeopardizing the family bonds, then there is no harm in doing so. Do not, however, divorce your thinking too far from the "tribe," and all that is therein implied. The human race is *not*, in fact, "one community" in any viable sense. Those who argue the contrary are merely playing the role of the cosmopolitan—either that, or you are deeply confused about this issue.

3

Never underestimate the value of careful observation. You will learn more by watching, listening, and experiencing the outer and inner worlds with a clear mind than you will ever learn by talking, or by trying to demonstrate your intellectual prowess to others. Acquire understanding as best you can, and put it to use in the rectification of your character and behavior. Displaying your understanding to others is a secondary interest—and not an especially admirable concern at that. The proper purpose of observation and inference is not gaining accolades or winning trivia contests. The mind is not a showpiece. Do not be so foolish as to pose in the guise of a sage. You are nothing of the sort.

4

Choose your role models and exemplars carefully. Do not trust the common perception, or received wisdom, about "heroic" figures. Some are deserving of their status, and some are charlatans who deceived their contemporaries, as well as credulous students of history. Not every idol is worthy of your admiration, and none warrant idolatry. Socrates, Diogenes, Epictetus, Marcus Aurelius, Buddha, and Jesus were all purveyors of values and virtues that have earned your respect and admiration. The sages, themselves, were arguably flawed in a variety of ways, and you, of course, never met any of them. You only "know" what has been recorded of their exploits and their teaching. How much of the legend is accurate in each case? You cannot know. You *can*, however, put their *counsel* to the test, and directly experience the consequences both within your own mind, and between those who claim to be devotees. How do they conduct themselves in imitation of their (alleged) exemplars? Do they seem ennobled by this emulation? Does it seem sincere? More importantly, have *you* improved by dint of their teaching? To the extent that you have *not*, is the flaw within you, or is it a product of some defect in the worldview you seek to embody? This is one of the central difficulties for any genuine acolyte. Whence the imperfections?

5

Entertainment as escapism is, for you, a waste of time. From what, precisely, are you in such dire need of "escape" that you spend hours in flight from reality as it stands directly before you—and within you? Your life does not merit this level of aversion to the direct, clear-eyed experience of it. For some, escape is an understandable impulse. Consider the prisoner, the slave, the oppressed, the "unfortunates" of whatever stripe you might care to mention. There is no dearth of horrors to contemplate. This world has never lacked for miseries to observe and experience. Some are, indeed, beset with challenges that might very well prove too much for the likes of you. The "wretched of the earth" can be absolved of the "sin" of escapism. For *you*, however, it is cowardice. For you, the term "sin" might be aptly applied. To have been granted so much, and to have accomplished so little with your advantages, a case can be made that this is shameful. Luckily, time has not quite run out for you. It *will*, of course. What do you intend to make of yourself between now and then? More than good intentions are required now.

6

Do not insist upon greater reward than an endeavor can plausibly offer. Fulfillment and happiness cannot be the object of every pursuit. Do not anticipate heightened emotional, psychological, or spiritual experiences to ensue from trivial, quotidian tasks and chores. Take out the trash. Do not expect to attain enlightenment on the way back from the curbside. This does not suggest that enlightenment is unattainable, or even that it cannot be had by emptying a dustbin with proper care and attention. The counsel here pertains to expectation. Perhaps even more so, it pertains to the insistence that certain moments *must* be filled with magic or wonder. Sometimes, just breathing in and out is wonderful enough.

7

Keep your body reasonably clean and healthy, but do not obsess about such matters, and do not agonize over your physical appearance. The body is a tool kit. Keep the tools in working condition as best you can, but do not concern yourself with the indications of ordinary wear. A pristine tool has probably been put to insufficient use. Your scars, your greying hair, your broken bones, and all the areas in need of maintenance are just signs that you have lived viscerally as well as within the confines of reason. You have not shied altogether away from danger, but you are no hero either. The world is a rough and bumpy place, and no one gets out entirely unscathed. This is as it should be. A life entirely devoid of injury is a life half-lived at best. Imagine that you had never been punched in the face, tackled roughly to the ground, or subjected to the various lacerations attendant upon collision with immovable objects. What a shame that would have been. Pain is an efficient instructor.

8

Money has its legitimate uses. You should not deny this, nor should you attempt to make a show of some imaginary disdain of the pecuniary. Money is, however, merely an instrumental good. Utility is the sole virtue of the stuff. In and of itself, money makes you no wiser, no more virtuous, and no more admirable, than does any other instrument. Do not envy those who possess more of it than you, and do not pity those with less. You can discern nothing about character, integrity, or self-respect in a ledger or bank account. On what account do you shun the homeless or the penniless? What did Diogenes possess? Where did Socrates hide his riches? Did the Buddha carry a golden alms bowl? Did Jesus offer the Sermon on the Mount from a palace? In their names, the world has been offered priceless benefits—but this has not been accomplished without a price. The virtuous *use* of money is the key. In the absence of judicious management, money may as well be used for a bonfire.

9

Find something before which you may sincerely humble yourself. This is not a difficult task. Both the material world and transcendent reality (if it *is* reality) offer grandeurs from which you may readily choose. Do not, however, *feign* humility or reverence merely because the masses or the mighty insist that you ought to do so. Disingenuous self-effacement is an insult to both the object of your phony reverence and, perhaps as importantly, to yourself. Indeed, if it is false, the modesty expressed becomes a kind of self-aggrandizement—a show to win the acceptance or approval of some audience. There is no need for playacting. There is no justification for taking up some fraudulent veneration or sham devotion. The world provides ample resources to engender genuine awe. The voices of majesties call out from every direction. You need not listen long to perceive one calling *your* name. Indeed, you have to stop up your ears to *avoid* hearing. Be still a moment and attend to the voices.

10

Who are you that anyone should heed *your* counsel? Indeed, you have not even earned the right to *keep* your own counsel. There are simply no alternatives available in some areas of endeavor. You have had to find your own way, and have failed to do so at least as often as not, because no one felt compelled to bother with you or your interests. Can you blame them? Were you anyone else, how much attention would you pay to some lost soul of *your* stripe? On what grounds would you spend the effort? What hope do you believe you engender in any who encounter you? If there is evidence that you are something more than an awkward, dysfunctional, talking ape, you must admit that this evidence is remarkably well concealed. Nothing about you appears special or worthy of particular notice. Therefore, do not flagellate, even in your own mind, those who ignore your advice or disdain your counsel. There is nothing inherently unreasonable in their indifference to your opinion. Respect, as you well know, must be earned.

Book VI

1

Are you really so foolish as to regard your opinions with some special degree of reverence? You have been proven wrong more times than you care to count. You can scarcely imagine being further removed from infallibility, yet you sometimes cling to your cherished beliefs with an unholy zeal utterly unsupported by the available evidence. Grow up! Admit that you are no one special. Do not pose as the Oracle at Delphi. If you are *asked* your opinion, and *only* if you are asked, then you may offer the most carefully considered assessment of which you are capable. Whether your words are heeded, ignored, or ridiculed, it is of no proper concern to you. It is inappropriate to attempt to impose your will upon others by fiat, or by any form of coercion. Let people live their own lives, make their own decisions, and experience the consequences of having done so. Your commentary on those consequences is not for public consumption.

2

Never lose your love of the written word, and maintain gratitude that you had the opportunity to develop this edifying habit. You can hardly imagine your life without access to books, ideas, information, and all else that is conveyed in writing. For you, an unlettered life would be at least half a life thrown away. Literature is to be cherished. Explorations within the sciences, philosophy, and the other humanities have enriched your life in ways that defy calculus or quantification. The Stoics, especially the Romans, have shown you a way of life, a system of values, and methods of practice without which you would almost certainly have devolved into wretchedness. Scriptures from the world's major religious traditions have suggested possibilities without which you would probably have fallen into barren hopelessness. Scientific works have opened your eyes and your mind to the almost unfathomable grandeur of the natural world, its laws, and the place of humanity within it, without which you would almost certainly succumb to anthropocentric aggrandizement that you now believe to be an absurd delusion and all too common embarrassment. Books have taught you something about knowing your place. This is a very valuable lesson.

3

What is it that troubles you? In considering that question, do not make the mistake of searching the external world and events transpiring therein. The world will have its way. To insist that it should be otherwise is to insist upon what has never been and can never be. It is the petulant desire to have your preconceived attitudes confirmed, or your stubborn wishes fulfilled, and it leads inevitably to frustration and discontent. Your *mind* is your greatest challenge. Focus your will and your efforts on the rational rectification of your desires and aversions. Know that a desire frustrated, or an aversion incurred, is evidence of flaws in *you*, and not evidence of a flawed or unjust world. You have only yourself to blame for your dissatisfaction. Who are you to demand that events should conform to your whims? Do not be ridiculous.

4

Do you find that your faith is shaken? If so, do you regard this as evidence of a flaw in the object of your faith, or do you detect a dysfunction in the nature and practice of your faith itself? Perhaps your faith is misplaced. Perhaps your perception of circumstance is inaccurate or misguided. Perhaps your expectations are irrational or unrealistic. Perhaps the manifestations you anticipated are not those to which events are, in fact, susceptible. Consider the possibility that your faith wavers because of flaws in *you*, and because of *your* failure to calibrate your beliefs and expectations wisely. Be assured that God is *not* the problem. God is either a fiction, or the author of the cosmos. In either case, you are in no position to register complaints concerning the ways of the world. If your life is a malignancy, you have no one to blame but yourself.

5

There is far too much noise and chaos in your life, is there not? Do you attribute this to a "world gone mad"? If so, you abrogate your responsibility to maintain rational equanimity irrespective of circumstance. A "mad" world is no excuse for your failures of self-discipline, and it is certainly no excuse for you to join in the alleged madness. Do not absolve yourself of your duties as a rational agent endowed with the capacity to adapt, control your actions, and govern your mind in felicitous fashion. The world itself is not a proper object of blame or disapprobation. Persons inhabiting the world are either doing their best, or they are not. Either way, who are you to cast aspersions? Do not set yourself up as a font of wisdom. You are nothing of the sort. You are a wellspring of mediocrity and complaint. Set about changing *that*.

6

Everything must pass away. This is no reason for histrionics or despair. Events transpire, objects transform, and then they are no more. Would you prefer moments frozen in time? If so, you underappreciate the future and its possibilities. You also neglect the present, and its immediacy in your experience. You are here *now*. That is enough to make a start. Do you fear your own passing away, or regard your efforts as pointless merely because you are not immortal? Is so, you overvalue yourself and under-value the life that you have been granted. Who are you that you should not share the common fate of all those who have come before you? The world has no special need of you, but you are, quite literally, nothing without it. Do not turn yourself into an idol or an object of your own ludicrous reverence. That is nothing more than vanity. You know yourself too well to believe that the world will be diminished by your departure from it. Do not foolishly crave a longer life than you are allotted. The time granted you is more than sufficient. Remember that you did nothing to *earn* your existence. You look the gift horse of the present in the mouth to your own detriment. Your life is now — and that is enough.

7

There is something silly about your aspirations. Is your career worthy of special note? Have you produced any work without which the world could not readily make do? Endeavor to see your contributions in the broad context by which they are dwarfed to insignificance. Do your best, but do not deceive yourself that your efforts are indispensable. Do not fall into the many traps set by your ego. You are small, ephemeral, and of no momentous account. Before long, you will be dust, and everything about you will be forgotten. If even *you* cannot maintain humility, then a ridiculous creature wastes its time and makes a fool of itself until you finally drop dead. *What* do you think you are? A yammering ape, hurling its feces about its cage, is not a lesser being than you. Indeed, this creature at least shows no signs of your undeserved arrogance. Perhaps it has the better of you.

8

Always afford others the fairest hearing that you can manage. Avoid contempt as far as is, for you, possible — and work diligently on expanding your forbearance in this area. Do not "smirk" internally when those with whom you initially disagree explain their point of view. You are no less fallible than they are. If you are honest with yourself, you must admit that you have found yourself on the wrong side of the debate more times than you would wish to admit in public—or even to yourself. Your unwarranted self-regard is both unbecoming and worthy of punishment, if anyone is paying attention. Do not expect your condescension to be forgiven. Even an imbecile can smirk. You are all the evidence needed to verify *that* particular claim. Listen more humbly. Smirk less. Do not make an ass of yourself.

9

Never fail to appreciate the unearned opportunities that you have been granted. Relative health and a moderately well-functioning intellect could easily have been denied to you. Indeed, you have slight grounds for assuming that they were *not* denied you. These are gifts not provided to all. Remember also that others are endowed with them in far greater measure than you can hope to attain or emulate. Genuine gratitude is incompatible with arrogance. What you have is enough. What you lack is more than enough to maintain an abiding humility—or *should* be so. What others have been granted is none of your concern. What others lack is not a legitimate object of your disdain. Furthermore, you can never be certain about what abilities are granted to, or denied to, others. Indeed, you are far from certain about your own faculties and alleged prowess. Be slow to judge another's abilities. There *are* humble geniuses in the world.

10

Watch your temper. Decisions made in anger seldom culminate in desirable or praiseworthy consequences. You have made far too many mistakes because you have allowed your irritability to get the better of you. These errors have impacted others in ways that you now regret and, moreover, they have diminished *you* by your own lights. Do not, yet again, shame yourself in a moment of ire. A rational hesitancy to anger is a trait common among all of those whom you admire most deeply. Socrates withstood the bitterest shrew of a wife in all of Athens, and bore the ridicule of half the masses with good humor, abiding calm, and searching self-reflection. You are, to be sure, no Socrates. You are not fit to hold the hem of his tunic out of the dust. You *are*, however, obligated to emulate his example as best you are able—pale though you are fated to be by any such comparison. Either improve your self-control in this area, or admit that you have never been sincere in your aspirations. Are you in earnest? Act like it. Prove it.

Book VII

1

How many times are you going to allow yourself to commit the same error for the same reason? Are you not ashamed of falling prey to the same weaknesses time and time again? You are well aware of most of your vulnerabilities, yet you have devoted inadequate effort to rectifying your worst and most inveterate habits. You must be more responsible and diligent about self-discipline, if you hope to make any real progress. It is simply not enough to contemplate these matters from time to time, or to exert an occasional effort. You are like someone who periodically goes on a diet, only to revert, again and again, to junk food and beer. The meagre progress you make, or *seem* to make, disappears as you regress and fall back into the old patterns of behavior. Discipline must be *sustained*. There can be no "time off for good behavior." Vigilance!

2

Keep your ego in check. Make no attempt to display your supposed prowess to others. This is an indication of weakness and insecurity. The impulse to impress persons for whom you have no particular respect is worse than weakness—it is perversion. Appealing to persons of low character is certainly no path to virtue and decency, and the very attempt to do so reveals all too much commonality between you and your audience. Do the best you can for the sake of so doing. Do not make a show of your efforts or talk too much about what you aim to do, or why you aim to do it. Attend to your own character, and leave others to attend to theirs. If your efforts are for show or display, then you have made no real progress. You are like a juvenile shouting, "Look at me! Look at me!" Adults do not crave attention.

3

Laughter is said to be good medicine. If so, laughter at one's own expense is one of the finest tonics for those ills stemming from inordinate love of self—and this is surely the most fecund source of dysfunctions afflicting your character. What is this bizarre obsession with yourself? How many times can you read your own words, inspect yourself in the mirror, or tell tales of your exploits and experiences? Why this impulse to sell your story to the world, as if you have accomplished something noteworthy? All the times you have enjoyed laughter at another's expense, it should have occurred to you that *your own* conduct cried out for derision. Your flaws are, indeed, a laughing matter. It is better to embrace this fact than to maintain delusions of superiority. You cannot, with a straight face, sing your praises any longer. Your life is, at best, a comedy.

4

Do not increase, beyond necessity, the number of secrets you feel compelled to keep. If you engage in behaviors that you would not want others to know about, it is probable that you do some disservice to other persons and to yourself. It is not your business to reveal anything told to you in confidence, and trust is well worth cultivating. Keeping secrets about *yourself* is, however, a sign of weakness or worse. What have you done that must be concealed? Why have you behaved in such contemptible fashion? Just how much, do you suppose, have you concealed from *yourself*? Rational adults do not conduct themselves in disgraceful fashion. Honest adults do lie to themselves, or others, about who they are and what they have done. Are you neither rational *nor* honest? Consider the secrets that you keep, and you will have an answer.

5

Do not take pleasure in the misfortunes of those whom you

dislike—and reason carefully about the grounds for your assessments of those for whom you experience distaste. Even if your attitude seems well founded, however, this does not justify a petty disposition regarding difficulties or setbacks suffered by others. Pettiness does suit you—or so you ought to hope. *Schadenfreude* is hardly a foundation for your advancement. How small you are when you revel in the failures of others—especially given your own penchant for malfunction, fiasco, and miscarriages of decency. When you are able to chuckle sincerely at *your own* misfortune, *then* you will have made progress. Until that time, remember that you are no better than those you behold.

6

Propaganda is effective for narrow, poorly developed minds. Unfortunately, propaganda *is* fairly effective. Thus, one cannot help but wonder about the qualities shared commonly among the masses. The great defect of democracy is precisely its alleged virtue. The masses get to vote, whether they have any understanding of the issues at hand or not, and no one person's vote carries any more weight than any other. The masses are, ostensibly, in charge. You should not expect wholesomeness and wise policy to ensue. This is, however, no justification for complaint. If the voters choose poorly, and they often will (have you *not* had cause to regret *your* choices?), then a rational adult must adapt, rethink, and respond to the political realm as it *is*—and not as one might insist it "should have been." The world is enough as it is. There is no great benefit in obsessing over counterfactuals.

7

Those who boast tend to suffer for it at some point. You are intimately familiar with this experience, are you not? Scripture tells us, for good reason, that pride precedes a fall. You have beheld the spectacle of smug, self-important nitwits humiliated through their own arrogance. Indeed, you have had more than one occasion to experience the humbling effects of your own childish immodesty. Yet, your pride persists. It seems that you learn only at great length, and at the expense of significant suffering. Somehow, your vanity endures. Of course, it is worth noting that the humble can plummet and tumble as well. So, while pride may go before the fall, humility may also precede a downfall. Somehow, however, the collapse of the proud feels more like justice.

8

The planet swarms and teems with living things. What, if anything, distinguishes one life from another, or makes one living thing more significant than another? Intellect appears to be an advantage. Is it, however, a *moral* superiority? Perhaps it is. A case can be made for saying so. Should you, therefore, revere the genius more than your own middling mind? Perhaps you should. Has Einstein not provided the world with far greater benefit than you ever could? Should you, therefore, disregard the plight of the dim-witted—and assume that you are not properly numbered among them? But for the grace of God, heredity, or happenstance, you could well have become a mental deficient. By the way, just how confident are you about such grace? A pause and at least a few moments of reflection are called for at this point.

9

What is, at root, not attributable to either dumb luck or provi-dence? Life itself is either a gift or a happenstance. Innate faculties and initial environment cannot be claimed as achieve-ments. No one *earns* innate genius, athletic inclination, or initial capacities. From these, you have derived the rest of your experience and abilities—paltry though these latter may be. Had your mother fallen down a flight of stairs while you were in her womb, it is altogether likely that injuries or trauma to your fetal skull would have precluded even those scant accomplishments

44

that you have managed. A genetic "glitch" might have rendered you an imbecile or a cripple. Your childhood could, quite easily, have proved a far more damaging ordeal. You have witnessed such afflictions in others. Perhaps some of these others perceive defects in *you* of which you are unaware. Be mindful that you are merely acting a part in a play that is not of your devising. Your character need not have appeared in "the script" at all.

10

While you are well aware that you have been wrong on many occasions, you must not ignore or discount those times that you have been proven correct. You are certainly fallible, but not unfailingly so. Even a fool stumbles into the light now and again. A degree of circumspection and intellectual humility is healthy and wise. Chronic, incorrigible self-doubt, however, is stultifying and unwarranted. Do not assume that your detractors are wrong, but do not assume that they are always correct either. Sift through the available evidence as best you can. Investigate the matter at hand as assiduously as the subject merits. When the time for choosing arrives, you must act. You must be decisive, you must commit, and you must devote yourself to the goal. Of course, you may periodically reassess your position and your reasoning. Admit your mistakes when you make them—and you *will* make them. Do not, for this reason, allow yourself to become paralyzed with indecision. This can be a form of cowardice. Condition yourself to move forward into the fray. You need not know *everything* in order to do *something*.

Book VIII

1

Do not be swayed by the mere opinion of the masses or the majority. The truth is not determined by plebiscite. The planet was not flat when nearly everyone believed it to be so. It has always revolved around the sun, even when this was not widely understood. Do not retreat from an unpopular position merely because it is unpopular. Adhere to the dictates of reason and evidence as best you are able. You have no obligation to agree for the sake of being agreeable. You have no obligation to allow yourself to become merely another voice among the multitudes. There is no special virtue in this type of conformity. Galileo was not willing to be consumed at the stake, but he seems, in the long run, to have prevailed in the debate. Pursue the truth wherever it leads you. Do not expect applause for this.

2

Few, if any, of your heroes were embraced by the masses in their own time. Some are reviled or disregarded to this day. Your admiration must be based upon virtue, wisdom, and strength of character. It must not be contingent upon popular appeal, as this is no evidence of excellence. Emulate those you admire. Ignore the bleating of the herd. Diogenes was mostly regarded as a madman—and not without some justification. He was not, due to a general disapprobation, deterred from his style of life, or his devotion to simplicity, honesty, and freedom from convention. Where is your courage to defy the norms and mores that you find repugnant or silly? What are the limits of your adherence to principle? Until you are tested, you cannot know your fortitude. Do you *want* to know?

3

Everything you valued in your youth is dying. This is both literally and metaphorically true. You have lost a parent, a sibling, friends, and beloved pets. The world has retrieved these—as all were "yours" only on a kind of loan. More is to be reclaimed. The collapse of your nation appears to be irreversible. A culture bent on suicide can only be saved if it is shaken out of its moribund haze. You see no sign that this is at all likely. The only rational course of action is a radical cognitive restructuring. If you allow your peace of mind to remain fastened to an imploding, self-immolating nation, culture, or some conception of a future that is incompatible with the present, then you assure yourself a misery persisting unto death. This *is*, it should be noted, an option. It is not, however, a reasonable choice—and giving in to despair is intellectually craven. Your mind and your life are not determined by the darkness of the age in which you find yourself embedded. You must be a light unto yourself. Most of the other lights, it seems, are flickering.

4

Should you not worry about your family and their welfare? Note that the worrying, in and of itself, does them no good and only serves to keep you ill at ease. Pay attention to challenges, dangers, and potential damage they may do to themselves. Offer your counsel when it is appropriate to do so. Offer your protection insofar as you are able. Keep your eyes, ears, and mind open to anything that might threaten their safety. Do not, however, insist that all must go well for them at all times. This is not the way of things. You will be of little use to your loved ones if you cannot maintain your reason and your composure when the times of testing arise. Wisdom requires an honest acknowledgement of human frailty and imperfection. Your family is not immune to suffering. Stay alert. Remain calm. Be decisive, and even brutal, when you must. More than this is beyond you. Keep mortality always in the back of your mind.

5

No obligation is to be taken lightly. If your responsibility pertains to a relatively small issue, it does not follow that your responsibility is, *itself*, an insignificant matter. Shirking any obligation diminishes you, and strengthens an unfortunate and disgraceful habit. Your character is your primary concern. Do not allow the entrenchment of weakness or indifference to intrude where your most fundamental obligations are concerned. A promise made is to be a promise kept. This is no mere platitude. If your word is not your bond, you have no business issuing assurances at all.

6

There is something hollow about the "intelligentsia" of your day, is there not? The punditry, the academics, the political leaders, and the rest who speak as if they do so *ex cathedra*, mostly strike you as disingenuous and corrupt. You cannot trust "conventional wisdom" or "common sense" in the forms you find in the media or the academy. Your job is to pierce such nonsensical façades and seek the truth. Attend to this obligation as if your breath depended upon it. It is a paltry philosopher who takes the "learned" at their word. Consider what Socrates did to the "great minds" of his day. What a shame if he had not been executed for it. A martyr to humility in the pursuit of truth is no trivial loss. His example stands before you. Do you intend to ignore it?

7

Tribalism is not to be underestimated, nor is it properly dismissed as inherently irrational or without merit. There are, to be sure, dangers associated with unwise collectivist impulses. The mob is a formidable beast. It does not follow, however, that all forms of association are equally dubious. Everyone feels a greater affinity for "their own" as they understand and define "their own," than they feel for those not recognized among their number. This is probably unavoidable. You must think carefully about who is properly deemed a member of your "tribe," or justly counted among your company, and on what grounds you determine such matters. Is this identification a mere function of habit, or of convention? If so, investigate the foundation of this convention. Subject the habit to rigorous scrutiny and analysis. In this area, as in all others, a bad habit is properly laid aside. A good tribe, however, endures. Rome has fallen, but the Jews persist.

8

It is best to accept a gift only out of respect for the benefactor. To accept a gift out of self-interest or greed is to value your dignity less than the item that you receive. Do not tell anyone that you would like such-and-such as a present, but tell everyone concerned that you are not in need of more material things cluttering your life. Suggest a grant to charity as an alternative to this sedulous accumulation of ever more "stuff." For those who insist upon tradition, accept their offering with grace and gratitude. Perhaps the gift answers some deep need to *give*. Do not deny anyone this satisfaction. Genuine generosity should not be met with anything that can be interpreted as ingratitude.

9

You have always distrusted various elements of the political process. Politicians rarely tell the truth, unless the truth happens to coincide with their self-interests or those of the party to which they have pledged themselves. Politicians do not seem to regard honesty as an intrinsic good. It has, evidently, always been thus with them. The choice is to desist in your participation in a corrupt process, or to continue to vote and assess issues, while accepting that your efforts are likely to have little or no impact upon the political realm. Voting for the "lesser of two evils" is still voting for evil. Where is the honor in that?

10

Anyone who values position and power more than truth clearly cannot be trusted with position, and clearly ought not to be granted power over the citizenry. Dishonest people should never hold positions of influence, yet honest people are seldom attracted to such positions. Honest people are well aware that governing themselves, and rectifying their character, is more than enough to occupy them for the full span of their lives. Those who seek to govern others often do so for the sake of exploiting the power's inherent political position. What are you to do about corruption? Clearly, you are obligated to avoid allowing yourself to become infected with this moral dysfunction. Beyond that, your efforts are unlikely to accomplish anything worth mentioning. Do not insist that political leadership *must* be more honorable than is possible or likely. In fact, do not insist upon anything at all pertaining to the external world. Insist upon *your own* honor and decency. That will have to be enough.

Book IX

1

Do not *loan* money. This is an invitation to conflict and resentment. If you need the money, do not part with it. Apologize for your inability to be of assistance, and try to direct those in need to a more viable source. If you *can* part with the money, do so in the form of a gift. Once the gift is given, you have no business ever thinking on the matter again. Any expectation of reciprocity taints the exchange. Avoid turning interpersonal relationships into another form of business in the marketplace. If you expect or demand future consideration from the current recipient or your largesse, you diminish yourself, the value of the gift you give, as well as the sincerity of the association. There is something vaguely coercive about such expectations, and something explicitly coercive about such demands. If you regard the matter at hand as strictly business, at least have the decency to admit as much up front. Give *freely*, or do not give at all.

2

At whom do you direct recrimination? Do you chastise the cheat, the liar, the hypocrite, or the charlatan? Do you imagine that any of them could have turned out other than they are? How so? Each of us is endowed with a hereditary allotment over which none of us has the slightest control. Each of us is faced with a set of initial circumstances to which we did not consent. Events transpire within and without our bodies, and these shape us neurologically, biochemically, psychologically, and in innumerable other respects that determine our beliefs, desires, aversions, attitudes, proclivities, etc. These all jointly culminate in decisions and actions. Character accumulates. Thus, one becomes a cheat, a liar, a coward, a hero, a stalwart, or what have you. What business is it of yours that someone else turns out in this way or that? Do you find insufficient need for improvement within yourself? Look harder.

3

You know that your time is limited. Neither you, nor anyone else, can guess how much time is afforded any of us. Assume that the end is nigh. Assume that you will not live to see your efforts come to fruition in the external world. Dispense with any concern regarding such matters. Your duty is not altered if you have much remaining time or little. Your business is the rational governance of your own mind and the improvement of your own character. When the end comes, let it find you doing your best. Greet the Grim Reaper with a clear mind and a steady gaze. Shake his bony hand if he extends it. Tell him that he caught you working on becoming a better version of yourself. What more is there for you to do? Should he ask if you are ready to go, tell him that you never believed yourself to be immortal.

4

Physical labor is not to be disdained, avoided, or accepted only grudgingly. The work of the hands, and of the body, is also work for the mind, and exercise that builds character along with muscle. Those who denigrate physical labor reveal their ignorance of complex psychophysical causal interactions. The body teaches the mind about the surrounding world. Sloth in this arena is worthy of contempt. A hard day's labor is a reward unto itself, and a day's labor lost is its own punishment. What labors did you neglect to engage in today? What accomplishments were lost as a result? You will not get this day back again. Waste too many days, and a life flows by before you know it. Do not take tomorrow for granted. You never know when you may be leaving to another some burden that was rightfully *yours* to bear.

5

Happiness is not a proper pursuit. If virtue does not entail happiness, you are to pursue virtue nonetheless. If virtue is, somehow, *incompatible* with happiness, your obligation is to pursue virtue *at the expense* of happiness. A good, but unhappy, man is a better human being than a happy man who fails to be decent, honorable, self-disciplined, and noble. Luckily, the evidence suggests that virtue is generally conducive to fulfillment, earned self-esteem, and contentment. Indeed, whatever degree of happiness is available within the human condition seems enhanced by virtuous behavior. Therefore, you are to make your best efforts to be a *good* person, and allow happiness to *ensue* as a matter of course. If being virtuous does not contribute to your happiness, this is evidence of some malformation of your desires and interests. If decency does not enhance your feeling of well-being, you may simply be indecent. If so, what business do you have being happy?

6

Emotional attachment to political, economic, or cultural affairs is all but guaranteed to produce recurring disappointment. Who, after all, gets the desired results at *all* times in these arenas? Renounce desire and expectation of any particular outcome in these spheres of human interaction. Withdraw your consent to be distressed over events that are determined by forces beyond your control. Take note of these matters, but do not rest your contentment upon this outcome or that. It is one thing to *observe* events, it something altogether different to root for a particular conclusion of the events you observe. You may prefer a healthier or more virtuous society than the one you get. Of what use, in that case, is your preference?

7

Be the most admirable role model that it is within your power to be. This may benefit those who look to you for guidance, but it is *certain* to ennoble *you*, and enhance your most sacred goal of pursuing virtue. Be a light unto others—for your *own* sake. What, after all, is the alternative? If you shirk your duty to make the most of yourself that you are able, then you will have made less of yourself than you could have. In what way is this a benefit to you, or to anyone else? What is the good of being bad? What is there to respect about mediocrity (or worse)? What is the purpose of your life, if you allow your life to unfold without rational governance? Anyone can eat food, sleep, excrete, recline, dawdle, and accomplish nothing in particular. Existing and *living a life* are two entirely separable enterprises. Can you show no one what the latter looks like? Do you not, at the very least, wish to show it to yourself?

8

If you are genuinely compelled, then resistance is futile, and distress about the matter is irrational. Simply do what you must. If you are *not* compelled, then what is it *against* which you exert yourself? Surely, it can only be your own desires, aversions, and reticence to engage in the project at hand. Resist unhealthy desires, and disavow those aversions that are without justification. If you are reticent about some occupation, ask what it is that induces this feeling. If the honest answer is that you are loath to work, or to place yourself at some risk, then crawl back into bed and resign yourself to an idle existence. If, on the other hand, you find yourself doing something distasteful, in the absence of any obvious compulsion, then stop and ask yourself why you behave this way. If you can identify no legitimate reason, desist. Are you unable to do so? Are you merely unwilling to stop yourself? This is nothing more than evidence of weakness and failed self-discipline.

9

You have met with disapproval more times than you can count. On each such occasion, you should consider whether the condemnation is warranted. If so, learn from it and make the requisite alterations to your behavior. Your detractor has helped disabuse you of some faulty belief, or encouraged you to break a bad habit. For this, you owe gratitude. Is the censure unwarranted? If so, learn the lesson that groundless disapprobation is nothing to you. Another person's misconception is none of your business. Should that misconception pertain to you, the matter is *still* none of your business. Have you been entrusted with everyone else's beliefs and judgments? By what power were you endowed with the obligation to manage the contents of minds other than your own? What arrogant nonsense! Do not distress yourself over some error in judgment that occurs outside the confines of your own consciousness. Surely, you have ample error within yourself to merit your full attention.

10

Do not pose as a sage. Epictetus would not even have allowed you to enter his schoolhouse. Socrates would not have kept company with you—unless he sought a bit of comic relief. The Buddha would not have wasted a robe and an alms bowl on you. Alexander would have cleft you in twain with a single stroke. Diogenes would have urinated on your leg and demanded that you thank him for it. No one is impressed with your piddling intellect, or your measly achievements. No one expects you to be a font of wisdom. You know yourself well enough to know what folly that would be. Your ego, if not held in check, is likely to be your undoing. Do not think too highly of yourself and your abilities. Compare yourself to *genuine* sages and persons of noble attainment. Acknowledge your inferiority before the "Council of the Wise," and do not pretend that you are a member of that august body. Who, after all, do you think you are? You barely command your own respect—and that only grudgingly and on rare occasion. Your arrogance does not even rise to the level of absurdity. Your ego is like a blowfish. It is puffed up as a false show of substance. How ridiculous you are.

Book X

1

You slide into bad habits over and over again. You appear to be an inveterate backslider, and you seem to subordinate self-discipline to whims, unhealthy desires, and passing distractions. Are you an adolescent? What is your excuse for this persistent failure? Is consistent decency "too much" for you, or are you just too little for it? A dog can be house trained in a matter of days. You, a (putatively) rational being, cannot train yourself to avoid stupidity and overindulgence with decades of life experience behind you? Pitiful. Get control of yourself before your time is done! How much time, by the way, do you think you have left? Mortality has a way of imposing limits without a great deal of advance notification. Procrastination is an abysmal strategy.

2

Violence is not always avoidable without resort to cowardice, or without shirking your responsibility to protect the innocent in your charge. When it is necessary, strike without hesitation or compunction. Strike to incapacitate as quickly as possible, and terminate the threat with brutal decisiveness. Be always prepared and always armed with appropriate means. Decisions made under duress are subject to dysfunction, and the mind and body tend to respond poorly to sudden danger. Make the most fundamental decisions *before* the critical moment arises. Act with urgency. Brutality may be called for. If so, be brutal. Kill if necessary. This is to be avoided if any viable alternative is available. If none presents itself, however, strike to kill. Sentimentality has no proper function in response to a clear and present danger. Be the wolf, not the sheep.

3

Enslave yourself to no man, no woman, no ideology, no theory, and no collective. Remember that selfish desire often binds you to unwholesome action. If you have the capacity to do something, then you *may* do that thing—though the entire world tells you otherwise. Of course, being *able* to do a thing does not, by any means, entail that you *ought* to do that thing. If you are forestalled by reason, by conscience, or by any honorable impulse, then the thing ought not to be done. Do not allow *external* forces to dictate to you what you will and will not do. Your actions are *yours* to choose, and you are responsible for them (or for omissions of action). Any law that can be broken is mere legislation, and nothing more than a human construct. Why obey legislation that you regard as unjust, unwise, or contrary to your principles? There are, to be sure, consequences for disregarding society's rules. Do you suppose that there are *no* consequences for abiding those rules that deserve to be broken?

4

Are you endowed with reason, or are you not? If not, then make a pig of yourself and pursue pleasure mindlessly. Better to be a happy swine than a miserable one. If, however, you are fortunate enough to partake of the gift of reason, then do not fritter it away like a fool, a child, or a dumb beast. If the primary utility of your reason is the satisfaction of desire and the pursuit of pleasure, then you are no better than a performing ape or a trained seal. Surely, there is more to a well-lived human life than food, sex, sleep, and entertainment. Toward what ends are you both willing and able to bend your will? Are these ends that improve the pursuer's character, or are these ends the stuff of mediocrity? It is well past time for you to leave mediocrity behind.

5

Are you "too hard" on yourself? Are you "overly critical" of yourself? Good. Better that than the reverse. You have seen the tragedy of wasted potential, and of intellect allowed to atrophy and wither until it deforms into idiocy. You have seen a decent man become a sluggard. You are to guard against wasting your paltry talents, as you would guard against a plague or a hostile invasion. Indolence in this arena is not worthy of forgiveness. Do not let yourself off the hook for wasting time and effort. You are not wise, but that is no excuse for slackening your resolve to become so. Get to work, and accept no apologies for your failure to make adequate progress. There is no viable alternative but to serve as a merciless taskmaster in your pursuit of the ultimate goal. You attain wisdom, or your life is a failure.

6

No task is too great to undertake. Many tasks are far too great for you to hope to accomplish or fulfill the prescribed goal, but none is so formidable that you cannot even set your sights upon it. Do not deceive yourself about your limitations, or use them as an excuse for faltering before you so much as take your first steps in the endeavor. A summit too high to surmount does not preclude an ascent as far as your abilities can carry you. You may not be able to scale Mount Everest, but you certainly have the capacity to sacrifice yourself in the *attempt* to make it to the top. Which do you find preferable, giving all you have in the effort to ennoble yourself, or giving next to nothing in the pursuit of comfort and an easy existence? If you prefer the latter, perhaps you ought to give serious consideration to the ease and comfort of the grave.

7

Many opponents are so formidable that you have no reasonable hope of defeating them. No opponent is so formidable that his prowess prevents you from facing him in the ring, the cage, on the street, or in any other arena of his choosing. You demonstrate respect for an opponent by preparing with every ounce of strength and every iota of resolve that you can summon. You then advance and contend against him with all of your might—until you are beaten straight through the floorboards. That is reverence for an adversary manifest in noble combat, even if it should culminate in defeat. Should you encounter some phenomenon against which there is no good reason to contend, then recognize that this is no proper opponent of yours. You are not to struggle against God, the laws of nature, or the world in which you find yourself. These are to be embraced, understood as far as your limitations allow, and revered as far greater than yourself. A *proper* opponent, however, is *never* to be feared. It is better to be destroyed in battle than to crawl before your adversary like a submissive dog.

8

Is *this* the best that you can do? Right now, this moment, this endeavor, and this level of effort are the facts before you. Is this your utmost striving? Do you tell yourself as much by way of excuse for your failure, weakness, and sloth? Perhaps a weak, lazy, miscarriage is especially susceptible to such "explanations" for mediocrity or worse. Pathetic. Set about your business like a *warrior*, or set a course for dissolution and self-destruction. What you are *today* is not worthy of any further consideration. Improve or lie down and await the inevitable. In fact, you might consider hurrying things along. You are not entitled to continue wasting time and space that might otherwise be filled by something of value. Get to work or drop dead already. This waiting room of a life is nothing more than a slow dissipation unto death. Move decisively in one direction or the other. This standing still is fit for no more than a mannequin.

9

Virtually every plot of earth, every natural resource, and every available means of sociopolitical control or economic hegemony has been claimed, disputed, and held out as a just cause of belligerence. Where has warfare not intruded into relations between this tribe and that? The psychotic, talking apes slaughter each other over land, gold, ideology, oil, and even the God that supposedly loves all of his children equally—so much so that apostates and unbelievers are to be subjected to forcible conversion or genocide. Has everyone forgotten that we all die in the end? Is there some great mystery about the terminal state of the flesh? We shall all pass away—and in not much time. This material world shall all pass away as well. Thus, let us wage war over every inch of it, and do so relentlessly until the end is upon us. Idiocy. There are causes for which it is necessary, and even noble, to fight. One cannot, however, plant one's flag in these.

10

There is either some absolute, invariant standard of good and evil, or all talk of "morality" is quibbling over a mere human construct. Why quibble over an invention of the mind? Let "them" have theirs, and "we" will have ours, and never the twain need meet. If there *is* an objective moral law, do your best to identify, understand, and obey it in *all* matters. Moral decency is second to no other interest. If humankind is to *invent* or construct a moral code, there is no discernible reason to adopt the one that happens to prevail in your particular time and place. The masses are as likely to botch the task of constructing viable rules of permissible conduct as they are liable to generate corrupt sociopolitical and economic systems. Look around you. Do you trust that what you see is the product of moral and intellectual exemplars? Does history provide any example of an ideal state or culture—outside the realm of fiction or a philosopher's imagination? If not, an absolute standard is at least as wisely chosen as any proffered alternative. A conjured morality will bind no one, settle no disputes, and can capture the hearts and minds only of the conjurers. If a law-giving God exists, He is not likely to look kindly upon those who seek to usurp his authority. If there is no such God, then why cede authority to another mere human?

Book XI

1

You are told *ad nauseam* what you "must" and "must not" say, "must" and "must not" do, what you "must" and "must not" believe, and what others "require" of you. Nonsense! No human being, and no collective, society, or subculture has legitimate authority to dictate your thoughts, words, or deeds. If you must suffer for speaking what you believe to be the truth, then suffer. If you must be punished for doing what you believe to be right, then embrace the punishment. It might be interesting to find your breaking point. Have you no curiosity about how much you can take? Those in power can take your job, your property, ruin your reputation, and end your life. They can lay it all waste with minimal effort. *None* of this is up to you. All of these matters pertaining to you, and to everyone and everything else, are bound to pass away in any event—and in not much time. Do not cling to concerns about them. Cleave to the governance of *your* will. In *this alone* are you indomitable.

2

Do you fear death? It is either the end of you, or it is not. If the former, then it is nothing to fear because the end of *all* experience is also the end of anything fearful. If the latter, then death *itself* is merely a transition to some other mode of being, or some other mode of experience. Thus, death should be no more terrifying than continued life and the experiential changes to which you have been subject for as long as you can remember. Fear death no more than you fear sleep, dreams, and the morning. Immortality in physical, human form is nothing worthy of your pursuit or envy. Indeed, it seems like a curse, does it not?

3

Self-pity is, in your case, despicable. Given the unearned advantages you have been granted, it is, at the very least, irrational. You have been provided with faculties, opportunities, and experiences, for which most of the world's population, and nearly all of its ancestry, would have gladly traded their limbs. Do not *dare* cry, "Woe is me!" with a straight face. Unless your complaints are an exercise in irony, they can only be an expression of loathsome boorishness and a callousness of spirit.

4

Are you owed an explanation? By what right do you insist upon it? Events occur as they will. No one promised you a hedonic playground or sustained joy. Did *you* set all this world in motion? Did *you* design the cosmos or impose the laws of nature? The planet turns, life scurries to and fro, rain falls, wind blows, creatures are born, and creatures die. It is not your place to demand to know the why and wherefore of *everything*. Indeed, *who could* owe you an explanation for any of it? If God made the world, and you, then *you* owe God an undying allegiance and reverence beyond measure. If there is no God, no Designer, no Creator, or any intelligence underpinning the universe, then there can be no one in a position to owe you an explanation of your presence in the world, the purpose of your life, or why you and your loved ones suffer. You are here, the point (if there *is* one) is uncertain, and you suffer because you are fragile and the world is a brutal place. No one gets out alive. *Earn* any further understanding you desire.

5

Cultivate appreciation. Your life springs neither from your hand, nor from your mind nor from your efforts. You appeared (as it were) in the world, and there are choices to make. It is either a gift of providence, or a byproduct of blind, unguided, natural processes. Every moment worth living is attributable to forces beyond your control. If you cannot muster gratitude for *that*, then you are a malignancy. At the very least, see that you do not metastasize and spread your discontent to other parts of civic body. The *very least* is, however, no effort to hold up with pride. The cure for your discontent lies within your own mind, and the medicine is administered only through the diligent application of your own will. If you lay the cure aside and decide, instead, to bleed yourself with leeches, do not then gripe about your discomfort.

6

Do not behave like a spoiled brat, claiming entitlement to every passing glittery object of potential amusement. Do not whimper about difficulties, and do not whine that you have been denied this, or that you have incurred that. There is no such thing as a *right* to satisfaction, or a legitimate claim that life must take one course as opposed to another. If events are contrary to your desires, you had better alter your desires and reexamine your aversions. Are this life and this world "not good enough" for you? Well, who are *you* to cast aspersions against reality? You simply emerged into this. You did not *merit* your way. The time, place, and circumstances of your birth are not accomplishments on *your* part. Do you reject this moment and your place in it? Do you *insist* that it *must* not be so? Fine. Go back to the beginning and start the whole thing again. Oh, you have no power to do so? Whine about your impotence then.

7

Keep needless expenses to a minimum. Some day you or someone for whom you bear responsibility will, almost certainly, face a significant, unforeseen expense. Material resources are finite and not easily replenished. Do not fritter away assets that are likely to be needed desperately in the future. Health fails, natural disaster strikes, emergencies appear as if they have fallen from the sky, and people that you love are going to suffer in ways no one predicted. Lacking resources because you have been prodigal is both humiliating and, more importantly, indicative of selfishness, childishness, and poor planning. Do not degrade yourself for an expensive meal, or some idiotic trinket. Do not trade a measure of security for a short-lived, unnecessary self-gratification.

8

It is, for all practical purposes, impossible to avoid passing judgment on others. Perhaps a vow of silence would suffice, but even then your facial expressions would likely give you away. Furthermore, it is irresponsible to fail in your assessments of those who might harm, or otherwise trouble, your family or the innocent. Given the opportunity to see a real problem "coming down Main Street," you cannot be absolved of the responsibility to point it out and alert those in the path of destruction. Politicians and persons in power must especially be subjected to rigorous scrutiny. The *sin* is in believing yourself to be inherently superior to those whom you judge. That is the common error. Identifying a flaw in someone else is not tantamount to proving that you are less flawed, or that you are broadly superior. Indeed, you may be obligated to pass judgment against yourself, and alert those in your vicinity.

9

Your weaknesses are more pervasive and more acute than they ought to be. No one is perfect, but no one is, therefore, excused from the obligation of moving in the general direction of perfection—to the best of their ability to identify the correct direction. You are quite confident that you could have behaved better and more nobly on many, *many* occasions. Your thoughts are *far* more unruly than they would have been had you disciplined your mind more assiduously. You could have done better. You could have *been* better. You are not. You are deeply flawed, and a far lesser being than you had hoped to become. What was the wiser expenditure of your time and energy that detracted from your self-rectification? You will acquire nothing of greater value than wisdom and virtue. Do you really know this, or is it mere pretense? An outside observer cannot have much confidence about the matter.

10

Conceit is an ugly and irrational state of mind. You believe this, yet you are *far* from free of this dysfunction. How often have you thought yourself superior in intellect, in physique, or in moral rectitude than some "poor wretch"? This is a compound perversity. Are these attitudes not, at root, directed at self-aggrandizement? Is this not indicative of insecurity? Every time you contemplate your "superiority," you verify your inadequacy. A genius does not need to make a show of, or spend much energy considering, an obvious intellectual superiority, any more than a giant needs to convince others, or himself, of his vastly loftier height. There is no evidence to suggest that lions feel compelled to take special note of their predatory prowess by comparison to lambs. Do not convince yourself that you are a lion merely because you spot a lamb. The lambs, after all, can also see each other.

Book XII

1

A member of your immediate family committed suicide. This is a fact, and it cannot be reversed. There is nothing unique to you in this event. This is something that happens. All the other suicides were simply not related to you. You did not pay them any particular mind, did you? Remember how outraged you were that the world did not stop turning, and that people just went about their business as if nothing had happened. From their perspective, of course, nothing *had* happened. What is your family to them? What is theirs to you? Hypocrisy was the source of your outrage, was it not? *Your* family had suffered an acute trauma. *You* had suffered. Your pain matters! Everyone should recognize this. Yet they all just keep breathing in and out. How long will you allow yourself to mourn? What good does the continuation of this behavior and state of mind do for yourself, the rest of your family, or anyone else? The world is a pitiless place. You have long known this. Do not suppose that there are limits upon the suffering to be endured. Your job is to endure. What is the good of calling upon others to endure trauma that is not theirs? Their suffering does not diminish yours.

2

Aging is nothing more than nature taking its course, and nature has probably been kinder to you thus far than you had any reason to expect. You expected more arthritis pain by now. You have never been terribly confident about your psychological stability either. The Sword of Damocles has hovered over your head since long before you understood the reference. Somehow, you have not yet broken down—not quite all the way. It seems that you are faring reasonably well. This is not to suggest that there is anything impressive about you, but only to note the very common cruelty with which the world afflicts us all. Your time will come, of course. For all you know, it may come long before you actually expire. Try not to get too comfortable. You have no idea when, where, or in what manner the bottom will drop out.

3

What kind of person struggles so mightily just to behave in a fashion that others find barely tolerable? The questioning and second-guessing of your words and deeds seems nearly ceaseless. How many mornings will you wake up and try to discern whether you have, or have not, needlessly alienated someone due to the previous evening's conversation? Admit that you take a perverse satisfaction in saying things that most people would prefer not to hear. You enjoy writing things that confound the reader. You often seek to be misunderstood, or understood only partially. Why this impulse to shock and push the limits of civility? Why the frequent resort to sarcasm, irony, and double entendre? Perhaps it is a manifestation of insecurity. Perhaps you find it comforting to hide behind semantic trickery. You have no good excuse for that. Grow up. Say what you mean, but do not speak for the purpose of meanness.

4

Sleep often comes to you only with significant difficulty, and sometimes not for the whole night. It is no simple matter for you to allow the stream of consciousness to wind down for the evening, lay your head upon the pillow, and switch off for rejuvenating rest. Imaginary conversations fill your head, as do imaginary deeds, and imaginary adventures. It is almost as if sleep frightens you. Do you find reality so dissatisfying that you need to indulge in adolescent flights of fancy? If so, you have no one other than yourself to blame. There are techniques for moving from the wake to the sleep cycle. You even know a few of them. Learn to calm down when it is time for calm.

5

Nagging pains are not a legitimate reason for complaint—even when the whining is confined to your own consciousness. No one is entitled to live a life free of suffering. No one walks through this "vale of tears" unscathed. Who are you that you should expect or demand a carefree existence? How weak are you that aches and twinges distract you from your purpose? Complaints have no purchase in this arena. They do not make you wiser or more virtuous. Quite the opposite, in fact. Do not waste time and energy bemoaning the normal course of physical wear and tear. Your pain is insufficient justification for the attention you give it—and for the attention *not* spent where it is needed. Children can be excused for valuing and appreciating things improperly. You are no longer a child. Stop crying like one.

6

Scatterbrains cannot be trusted with any task worth undertaking. They will let you down every time you allow yourself to rely upon their efforts. You have understood this for many years. Placing your trust in unreliable persons will result in shoddy work, numerous avoidable errors, and these consequences will be *your* fault. Do not blame a nitwit for failure and incompetence. That is what nitwits do. Blame yourself for entrusting the job to an intellectual deficient, or for expecting better than mediocrity from such persons. If you expect a buffoon to perform like a virtuoso, you invite frustration and failure. Such invitations do not suit a life governed by reason.

7

Complaining about an insect bite is an indication of irrational petulance. Did you not know that insects are to be found just about everywhere? Were you ignorant of their propensity to bite and sting? Were you aware that you were outdoors? Did you not notice the sun, clouds, and trees all about you? When the inevitable occurs, only a foolish child whines about it. The rain will fall. The sun will burn your skin. Ice tends to be slippery. Where do you find cause for befuddlement in any of this? When you feel death approaching, if you are granted any advance notice, remind yourself that it is the universal terminus of the human condition (at least of the body, and perhaps the extinction of the self altogether), and depart with the dignity of an adult who expected this result all along. Between now and that final moment, stop complaining about mosquitoes.

8

Moments of solitude are available almost anywhere. You must only retreat into the citadel of your own mind, and engage with the thoughts and perceptions you find there. If you find that your mind is an unruly place, then you must first remedy that condition. Only then will your retreat be worth the effort. The engagement with the contents of your consciousness should be kept as direct and immediate as possible, without unnecessary inferences regarding the causes or consequences of this thought or that perception. Quietude is not well served by directing thoughts outward into the buzzing, bleating world around you. Be still for a few moments and pay attention to your mind and its inner workings. Make peace with the inner realm of your experience. This will pay dividends when the outer world becomes inhospitable. Lower the gate, move inside, and disregard "the barbarians" for a little while.

9

A river is a felicitous metaphor when it comes to considering the course of your life. It is ever changing, flowing, moving—yet its banks and bed are comparatively constant and stable. Your unique genetic code remains fairly constant. The body to which it gives rise changes, but it does so, for the most part, at a relatively steady pace. Thoughts, on the other hand, flow like water—

sometimes, in fact, they rush like rapids, or overwhelm you like a tidal wave. The mind itself evolves in response to the experiences of the body, and the thoughts flooding through it. Think of yourself as a river. The river does not resist the forces imposed upon it. The river finds its course within the confluence of powers pervading the surrounding world. The river does not struggle. The river does not desire. The river is not dissatisfied. The river is at peace, though it flows and moves ceaselessly.

10

You are a tiny stream in confluence with great rivers, flowing out to bays and deltas, bleeding into vast oceans, creating vapor and clouds that produce rain and snow, from which the headwaters are formed, and the stream is replenished. You are a miniscule microcosm of ever larger, perhaps infinitely larger, systems. The whole universe contains *you* as a particle of an insignificant globe, floating in an inconceivably vast ocean of space and time. Is this ground for celebration, or for despair? Is it grounds for feeling any particular way at all? You are about as close to nothing as it is possible to be, yet you are undeniably a part of everything that ever was or ever shall be. You are nothing special, and for your sake, the universe expands. Appreciate this. Find your place. Move along through the flow of events, and let the tide carry you where you are going. Though you may resist and struggle, you will still end up where the tide is taking you. Try to enjoy the ride, and do not make a nuisance of yourself. The world has things to do.

Book XIII

1

If you are not moving toward more virtuous states of character and a more finely tuned mind, then what is the value of your time and effort? Your adult life will have been wasted if you acquire no more wisdom than you possessed as a child. Perhaps you believe that a certain amount of wasted time and energy is permissible. Are you, then, *still* a child? Are you a mental defective? Where there is no intellectual progress, there can be only stagnation or regress. The goal of an adult life *cannot* be grey hair and slower reflexes. Middle age, and beyond, are filled with physical decline. The intellect is the only area in which you might be superior at the age of 65, as compared with yourself at 25. Are you disenchanted with the enhancement of your reason? If so, you shirk an obligation with each wasted moment, and every pointless indulgence. Your mind and your character are all you have left—those and, presumably, very little *time*.

2

What justification have you imagined to warrant hatred? Suppose that you have been wronged—and, by the way, who has *not* been wronged? Examine the matter, and identify the culprit. Is the cause of your distress the words or deeds of another? How so? These are actions and sounds over which you have no control. The sounds emanate from this other person's mouth, the actions are engaged in by this other person's body, and still other persons may hear, and may see. Does that description of the event involve *you* in any way? Do not say, "My character was maligned!" or "My reputation was damaged!" Your character is *yours* to control. No one else can make you into a liar, a cheat, a scoundrel, etc. As for your reputation, what has *that* got to do with *you*? It inheres only in the minds and judgments of others. Are *their* minds yours to control? Do not be absurd. Your umbrage is self-inflicted. Desist in your outrage. Renounce it. Relinquish it. Hatred will do you no good. Do you not know that hatred poisons the mind and afflicts the body? Set it down. The problem is, thus, solved.

3

Terrorism has become an all too common occurrence. The terrorists imagine that they destroy their victims. To be certain, the victims often die and suffer grave injuries. This type of victimization does not, however, *shame* the victim. There is no shame in death. It is the common lot of the living. The victims perpetrate no crime, and perform no vicious act. Their *character* is untainted. The perpetrators degrade and dehumanize *themselves*. Their victims, and their actions, are the instruments of the terrorist's own abasement. Death is the way of all flesh, and it is no more degrading at the hands of villains than as a result of illness or old age. The perpetration of evil in God's name, however, is the one sin that the *Torah* tells us, explicitly, God shall *not* forgive. This is the meaning of the reference to "taking the Lord's name *in vain*." Performing murder, and claiming to do so on the Lord's behalf, is, we are told, not tolerable to the Almighty. You are not to become what terrorists are. You are not permitted blood lust in God's name—even if there is no God. War must not turn you into a mere beast of prey.

4

Let the greedy and the worshippers of Lady Pecunia have their ill-gotten gain. It is part of their punishment. The thief remains a thief whether he is caught and punished or not. This is the heart of the doctrine of Karma in Eastern philosophy. The thief, the fraud, and the swindler may not "get what they deserve" in terms of prison time, or public censure—but they get the character with which they have endowed themselves. *That* is Karma. All of us become what we make of ourselves and, in the aggregate, we get the society that results from all of our actions. The economy is nothing to you but the movement of money and goods about the vast, sprawling marketplace. Some of the money is moved by cheats and thieves. If you are neither a cheat nor a thief, you are not diminished by the mere movement of money. How and why the money changes hands is no concern of yours. It is like leaves blown by the wind.

5

Has a thief made off with some paltry trinket or some cash you had been holding? Let it be so. Do not trouble yourself about where property now resides, or about who gets to hold it for a little while. You know that no one keeps such things forever. They follow no one beyond the grave. Now, the thief must look after what he has stolen—until it is taken back from him by other thieves, by officers of the law, or as a result of his death. Let him bear the burden of needless possessions. He has relieved you of a tiny nuisance and transferred concern for the matter to himself. What a generous act! Never think on it again.

6

Someone has maligned you. Someone has passed a false rumor and impugned your character. Someone has assaulted your reputation. That seems a sizable effort directed at a chimera, does it not. Suppose someone had impugned your pet unicorn. Is this worthy of a fistfight or a lawsuit? Some social construct or other has been reconstituted in some minds other than your own. What do you care which sounds people make with their faces, or which thoughts they choose to entertain? Have you nothing more substantial to occupy *your* mind? If not, you may as well join in the gossip and the rumor mongering. What you set your mind to is the clearest indicator of your true character.

7

Do not allow external events to dictate your state of mind. Train yourself to remain as calm and as reasonable as you are able, irrespective of circumstance. Fear, anger, and even hope can drive you to foolish forms of behavior, and misbegotten utterances. Ignoble motives, and shameful thoughts, tend to culminate in deplorable actions. These reinforce elements of your character that contribute to dissolution, degradation, and decline from which you are not likely to recover. Do not dig your soul's grave with irrationality and anemic self-discipline. Do not be bullied by your bestial impulses, or by the dark recesses of your mind, from which spring dishonorable thoughts and urges. The outside world cannot *force* you to disgrace yourself. If you are in possession of your faculties, your character is inviolable.

8

Marshall your resources with an eye to potential need. Your family will face challenges and obstacles that cannot be foreseen—in addition to the many that are readily predictable. You fail *them* if you fail to manage the wherewithal of reasonable material security. You cannot safeguard their souls (if, indeed, there actually *are* souls), you cannot directly rectify their minds on their behalf, but you can do your best to secure food, shelter, medical care, education, and the other physical necessities of survival and flourishing. You will, of course, need the cooperation of various elements of the external world, and none of these lie within your direct control. Your *efforts*, however, are entirely up to you. You can *try*, with every fiber of your being, to protect your family. Beyond that, the world will have its way with all of you.

9

Money is not to be loved or made into an idol, but neither is it to be despised or ignored. It is an implement to assist in securing temporary control of certain portions of the natural world, or useful items engineered from natural resources. Though *you* may suffer relatively little from a dearth of funds (at the moment), you are not entitled to presume that your loved ones are similarly immune to financial vicissitudes. Do not assume that everyone else shares your values and embraces your ascetic disinterest in luxuries. You are responsible for protecting real persons, not idealizations. Psychological and emotional attachment to things that are not necessary for the good life are, like it or not, quite common. If your loved ones were sages, they would have little need of your efforts. If *you* were a sage, you would also have little need of your efforts. Meet everyone where you find them, and not where you think they ought to be. Remember that *you* are *far* from where you ought to be.

10

No one has ever thanked the Lord, or fate, or good fortune, for becoming addicted to some drug or some substance that ultimately subordinated the will and the character to obsession with it. No one ever expressed gratitude for dissolution, decay, and degradation. There are, at this point, very few mysteries about the consequences of addiction and dependence upon synthetic, mind-altering drugs. They lead to death but, more importantly, they lead to deplorable behavior and self-abasement on the way to an ignominious demise. You are to have no truck with poisons that destroy body and mind. You are not permitted "experimentation" in this area. If any such temptation should arise, you are to expurgate it without hesitation. Tear it out, root and all, or you summon horrors that will follow you the rest of your days. For you, there is no such thing as "recreational" use of narcotics. What other people do with the stuff is none of your business, and you are not to cast moral judgment against them. You, however, *are* your business. Do not play games with your reason.

Book XIV

1

Your unhealthy and irrational inclinations do not seem to abate readily. How easily you are given to wrath, selfishness, and enjoyment of the suffering of those for whom you have contempt. This last is a rather large category, is it not? Like a malignancy, you return to these vicious habits of thought, even after you thought they had been excised, thereby polluting your character and reinforcing precisely what you allegedly hope to expunge. Do you *really* wish to cleanse yourself of these flaws? If so, why do you persist in their reinvigoration? It seems that it can only be depravity or weakness. Perhaps it is both. Do not excuse yourself in this matter, but redouble your efforts to make something decent of yourself. Remain vigilant where sickness of the psyche is concerned. Surely, you recognize that the greatest and most recalcitrant enemy lies within your own heart and mind. Waiver in this, and you invite desolation.

2

How much do you know about yourself, and how well do you know it? It is not a condition of *complete* ignorance, but neither is it a matter of thoroughgoing transparent understanding. You sometimes state your beliefs and values. You remind yourself about them again and again. You also occasionally catch yourself in actions or thoughts that transgress your stated beliefs and values. So, is the *true* tale the one that you tell yourself and others, or is it the tale told by your deeds? Should those who encounter you believe their eyes or their ears when the two tell divergent stories? Certainly, *you* ought to know the difference at least insofar as *your own* beliefs are concerned. Yet, you remain something of a puzzle, something of a mystery to yourself. Surely, you enjoy a privileged access to certain aspects of your own mental life. It is, however, equally certain that this privilege is limited. To what degree are you able to be honest with yourself, and to know your own mind? The answer is far from certain.

3

Do not be overawed by wealth, power, influence, fame, or the like. None of these is indicative of good character or nobility. Revere wisdom wherever, and in whomever, you may find it. Respect excellence in any person, in any act, in any element of the natural world in which it may appear. Diogenes was homeless and impoverished. Jesus disdained wealth and worldly power. The Buddha went to and fro with an alms bowl. Socrates had contempt for the marketplace and its trinkets. Mohammed was unlettered. Gandhi wore homespun, simple clothing. Epictetus was a cripple. Who are the wealthy and powerful by comparison with these? Of course, Marcus Aurelius was an emperor. Seneca was a man of riches and political influence. Confucius was a government factotum. Outward appearances are not to be dismissed out of hand, but neither are they to be taken as irrefutable evidence of character. Watch closely. Listen carefully. Do not be fooled by mere appearances.

4

Pointing to another person's peccadillos as a method of discharging or diminishing your responsibility for your own flaws is dishonest, indefensible, and cowardly. The pervasiveness of vice does not make it less vicious as manifest in *your* character and behavior. You are not absolved of responsibility to improve yourself and ennoble your character merely because your failings are commonplace, or because you behold in others that which you despise in yourself. The fact that there are murderers does not justify your participation in a homicide. Pointing the finger of blame is a manifestation of moral sloth and childishness. Concern yourself with *your* conduct. Do not be a busybody scouring the planet for vices that you can find in abundance within your own breast.

5

War will, quite probably, remain with us for as long as our species persists. This is, in and of itself, neither a good nor a bad thing. Those who instigate and wage wars are not yours to command or constrain. In judging what is good and what is bad, look always to your own mind and your own conduct. Reserve your judgment, first and foremost, for *that* arena. If others insist upon waging war, and they will, you are to take note and respond rationally, but you are not to lose heart, or cast judgment against persons you do not know, have not met, and do not fully understand. Do not, however, allow the state of war to penetrate too deeply into your assessments of humanity at large. Look through clear eyes. Most persons have not made war. Most who have, seem to have done so only reluctantly. War is *with* us, but it is not too close to the core of us.

6

Never allow squabbles about money to sow enmity within the family. If any such dispute should erupt, immediately concede any and all claims that you may have thought you had in the matter. It makes no difference that your claim is just, or that your kin may be motivated by greed or malice. If so, their punishment is self-inflicted. They have made the mistake of valuing money more than family. Do not disgrace yourself by fighting against your own family over something as paltry and insignificant as an inheritance, or control of some piece of property. You cannot hold yourself guiltless if you participate in a quarrel so base and ignoble—thereby sacrificing harmony within the family. Shame on you if you lower yourself in this fashion.

7

Do not accept ignorance as an excuse for damage that you may cause to other people or to their interests. You are obligated to be aware of the likely consequences of your behavior, and you must accept responsibility *even* for those consequences that could not have been anticipated. It will not do to say, "I never intended for *that* to happen!" People do not live in the world of your intentions or your imaginings. Own your actions *and* their results. To do otherwise is to indulge in a bit of mendacity. You do not expect everyone else to forgive the damage you have caused merely because the damage was unintended. If you inadvertently plow your car through a house, you know that you cannot simply drive away free of responsibility for damages. What you destroy, you are to replace — if possible.

8

Do not bludgeon those around you with excessive moralizing. Your disapprobation should be reserved primarily for yourself and your own transgressions. No one wants you constantly hounding them about their every flaw and failing. If your offers of guidance are appropriate, make them clear, and make them brief, but make them also as gentle as the subject matter permits. Do not repeat yourself unnecessarily. This tends to dull the impact of your words, and also sets up needless obstacles to future communications. Very few people respond to a message delivered *ad nauseam*. The expression is quite apt. Repetition becomes sickening at some point. Be as hard on yourself, and as relentless with yourself, as you like. Do not subject other people to similar treatment. They are not yours to govern.

9

Are you worthy of anyone's respect? The question does not concern whether you *are* or are *not*, in fact, respected — but whether you are *worthy* of it. Do not bother yourself about anyone's assessment of your character. Their thoughts are not your business. *Do* concern yourself, however, with the question of whether your character and your behavior *warrant* respect. Be a virtuous human being as best you are able. Do not demand or expect recognition for any efforts you make. Your virtue, such as it is, should not be for show. Do you respect *yourself*? Should you? Produce the justification for your assessment. Is it compelling?

10

Watch your ignorant mouth a little more often. Do not abase yourself by uttering stupidities, or by speaking in anger, or by trying to get a laugh at someone else's expense. Think about what you are saying and *why* you are saying it. Is it true? Does it need to be said? Are you saying it for noble purposes, or are you speaking from impure motives? Is it appropriate for *you* to speak in this manner, or is it someone else's place to give voice to the sentiments in question? Do not speak without *reason* (in both senses of the term). Consider all of the needless, valueless conflict that you have generated by running your mouth when you should have maintained silence. How many regrets of this type are you willing to endure, before you finally develop disciplined habits of speech? Just shut up a little more often and observe the results. You love the sound of your own voice far too much, and far more than your words merit. Who cares what you think?

Book XV

1

The company that you keep is at least as important as the food that you eat. Do not suppose that you ingest via your mouth alone. Your eyes and ears are conduits to the inside as well. Indeed, these are more important avenues of access than the mouth. The latter fills your belly, the former saturate your mind. The contents of your belly hardly constitute your virtue. Friends and associates can strengthen your resolve and contribute to your development, or they can distract you from your primary purpose, and lead you into foolishness. Choose wisely with whom you spend your time and share your thoughts. Those decisions reveal more about you than about your associates. If your friends are fools or miscreants, you cannot maintain your decency.

2

Attempting to reason with an imbecile or a liar is a fool's under-taking, and nothing of value is likely to result from the effort. Why then do you persist in this quixotic endeavor? Why do you keep presenting arguments and evidence to those who have conclusively demonstrated their lack of interest in the truth, or in honesty? Misplaced hope is hardly a legitimate excuse. How much inductive evidence must you compile before you finally admit that this project is as near to hopelessness as you will find this side of the grave? Every moment spent in the company of a blockhead is a moment wasted in a futile enterprise. Do not judge the imbecile too harshly, but do not continue to waste your limited time and energy trying to teach pigs to play the piano. Just let them be pigs. They cannot help it. Neither can *you* be better than you are.

3

There is little benefit in humiliating an idiot. In fact, the attempt to do so bespeaks a poverty of *your* spirit. It is your ego that prompts you to embarrass small-brained mammals in public. You seek the approval of some audience or other. You take all too much pleasure in this performance. Who are you to make sport of a mental deficient? Who are you to ridicule the slow-witted? They cannot help themselves—as far as you can tell. Asking them to be more honest is like asking them to be fleeter of foot, or taller than they are. You should not secure your hopes to their success. More importantly, where is the comparative wisdom that entitles you to belittle these people? Have you not been publicly humiliated on more than one occasion? Perhaps yours is the wit in need of chastening.

4

Forgiveness is of benefit to those who transgress against you, but it is of even greater benefit to you. Unburden yourself of useless enmity. Remember that we are all deeply flawed. Remember that you have transgressed more times than you can count. Recall the transgressions that you would have committed had you not been prevented by circumstance. With all of that in mind, forgive those who have, like you, made mistakes, gone too far, or fallen prey to common human weaknesses and bestial impulses. Let them off the hook, and allow yourself to release your bitterness with respect to them. Also, take a moment to forgive yourself as well. Has anyone done you more harm than yourself?

5

Learn to appreciate calm, quiet, serenity, and equanimity. Learn to embrace solitude. You are seldom more at ease than when you are afforded a moment of private peace after an extended period of compulsory association with crowds, or with those familiar to you only peripherally. Even small groups have a way of alienating you from your natural condition and your most composed state of being. Be still for a few moments, at least. Breathe in and out, with no other concerns or distractions. Your body is designed to be at ease in a quiet, safe environment. You are not made for extended periods of stress. Allow yourself to relax when the opportunity presents itself. Do not seek discomfort. It will find you, and you must be able to function properly when it does. Do not, however, chase after it.

6

If you make a vow or a promise, you are to keep your word — unless you are physically incapable of doing so. If you lack the capacity to keep your word, you have no business offering it in the first place. Treat every promise as a sacred oath, and a binding obligation. Your word is no small matter. Your decency is not to be lightly discarded. If you *can* keep your word, you *must* keep your word. Promise yourself that you will never break a promise.

7

If your actions do not command respect, you must not claim any *entitlement* to be respected by anyone — including yourself. Character tends to reveal itself, and it is especially apt to do so under duress. Be prepared to consider the possibility that an absence of respect is warranted in your case. Who, after all, are you to expect anyone's admiration? What are your accomplishments that merit approval, or esteem? Do not demand that anyone must regard you in this manner or that. Work as hard as you can to cultivate admirable character, and to behave like someone who might serve as a decent role model. Do not insist upon recognition for these efforts. Indeed, this insistence defeats its own purpose. Only a fool insists upon being regarded as wise.

8

Appearances are not to be embraced unreflectively or taken at "face value." It is not at all uncommon that the way things *seem* diverges dramatically from the way that things actually *are*. Avoid rushing to judgment about events, about other people, and even about yourself. Even when you find yourself pressed for time, you are still obligated to consider the available evidence as carefully as constraints allow. Do not hurry your assessment more than is necessary. Do not sacrifice intellectual humility at the altar of efficiency. Judgments made under duress should be no more than provisional. Revisit the matter at a later time, when you have the opportunity to sift more carefully through the initial appearances. Do not rush without necessity.

9

Victimhood is not a virtue. Indeed, in some cases, a victim brings the consequences down upon his own head through inveterate stupidity, or through insistence upon behaving like a helpless sheep. You are not excused from the obligation to plan and prepare so as to decrease the likelihood that you and yours will be treated as prey. You are well aware that wolves roam the quiet countryside. You know what the wolves want. There is more than just a little of the wolf in *you*, is there not? You know how predators choose their prey. Teach those who are willing to listen how to avoid looking like lambs waiting to be taken to the slaughter. No plan is perfectly reliable, and anyone can fall victim at just about any time and place. Do not use this as an excuse for laziness in the arenas of planning and preparation. If necessary, you may have to become a wolf yourself. Can you unleash that predatory spirit at will? If not, learn how to do so. The need will, almost certainly, arise.

10

You have no obligation to accept anyone else's conception of virtue, decency, or propriety. No one holds a patent on wisdom, or on applications of sagacity to circumstance. Your friends, your family, the academy, and the media are all susceptible to (at least) occasional dishonesty and misperception. No one is perfect, and no one has all the answers you seek. No collection of persons is infallible, and no society has ever been devoid of pathology and dysfunction. Do not be impressed by the opinions of the masses. Do not desist in your pursuit of virtue and decency merely because you are met with disapproval or rejection. Chart a course, choose a pole star, and set sail. Devote yourself, heart and soul, to the attainment of goals that you believe to be most noble. Be willing to alter course if you must, and if you realize that you have made a mistake, but do not simplemindedly follow the prevailing winds of your day or your culture. Do not place too much trust in "common sense." It has failed too often.

Book XVI

1

Find something that you are not willing to sacrifice for *any* purpose or any benefit. Let this be your guiding light in all matters, and let every decision conform to your determination to preserve this ultimate value. Commit yourself to a life bound to the principle that your highest aim is inviolable and must guide your every significant decision. Test all available options against this guiding maxim. Do not compromise the foundation of your virtue, or whatever you have identified as the highest good. Be prepared to test your chosen goal periodically, but do not relinquish adherence to it lightly. Organize all of your affairs around the one sacrosanct centerpiece. Watch how readily your choices begin to become both simple and obvious.

2

If a man puts a gun to your head and commands you to dishonor yourself, it is far better that he pulls the trigger than that you obey his command. Let him degrade himself by killing without justification. Do not abase yourself merely because you meet with a threat of death. Socrates would not depart from his pursuit of wisdom merely to avoid the hemlock. You are no Socrates, but you are to emulate his example in this matter. Dishonor is *never* a viable option. Let *no* threat impel you to disgrace yourself.

3

Cultivate simplicity. Be content with little in the way of possessions, entertainments, food, drink, and occupation. Be simple of character. Do not act one part for this audience, and a different part for that. Your guiding principles should be few and readily recalled—especially under duress. Speak with clarity and precision. Unnecessary complexity is a perversion and an invitation to miscommunication. Competing, and sometimes conflicting, purposes or interests make for a muddled and untrustworthy character. How is anyone supposed to take you at your word, or entrust to you any significant responsibility, if you allow your goals to drift, or to become caught up in periodic flights of fancy? Keep the rules that govern your behavior simple and reliable. In this way, you will make yourself dependable and trustworthy.

4

Keep your exercise regimen simple and consistent. There is no need for complicated equipment, and flashy technique is more likely to lead to injury than to improvement. Understand what is appropriate for your age, physical constitution, history of injuries, and the general wear and tear that inevitably attends decades of training. Do not be lax about your physical health, but do not exceed the limitations imposed by nature and circumstance either. Health and relatively smooth functionality are enough for your purposes. It is not as if you hope to become a professional athlete someday. Those adolescent dreams died many years and several injuries ago. Do not pretend to have a future in cage fighting or professional football. You train to be a Stoic philosopher and practitioner. That goal is lofty enough.

5

When you were young, you understood virtually nothing about yourself, the world around you, or what beliefs, values, and behaviors were noble, healthy, or wise. You knew virtually nothing of real value. Unfortunately, you remained ignorant of your true purpose as you slowly matured. To call yourself a "late bloomer" is something of an understatement. Indeed, it is not entirely clear that you have "bloomed" even today. Your current ignorance is enough to make anyone wonder what, if anything, you have been learning all this while. Do not dwell too much on the stupidity of your youth. The subject is simply too vast for the limited time remaining. Your *current* stupidity is a sufficient object of concern, is it not?

6

If you have something better to do, leave your current pursuits and go do it. Before you go, however, consider whether your current activities do not seem a proper usage of your time, primarily because you are not sufficiently attentive to, and appreciative of, their merits. Perhaps you are missing the value of *this* moment, and what you are doing in it, because you are not paying attention. Perhaps you fail to appreciate the present because, like a child, you are immature and easily distracted. Instead of sighing and rolling your eyes, attend to the matter at hand like an adult. Stop your whining and pining. What is this moment lacking? What is its alleged deficiency? Is the deficiency, perhaps, *within* you—and not a "gap" in the external world, or the events transpiring therein? The world "out there" is doing just fine. It shows no signs that it is dissatisfied with itself.

7

How small and insignificant you are. Consider the billions of years already elapsed, and the seemingly endless future. Your life is as *nothing* by comparison. By contrast with the vast reaches of the universe, and the enveloping ocean of time, you are less necessary than is a grain of sand to hold your home planet together. Yet, you still seem to take yourself quite seriously. Is there not something oddly indefensible in this? Perhaps you take yourself too seriously precisely because you know just how insignificant you truly are.

8

Do not offer your respect or your allegiance lightly or without rigorous testing. Such things are to be earned—or not granted at all. Also, do not confuse respect with mere civility. The latter is relatively simply and easily expressed. Even a dog can be trained to shake, sit, and speak upon command. Simple pleasantries of this nature are of no special concern and have no real purchase beneath the thin veneer of the social. Declaring your respect or allegiance is an enactment of association and an endorsement of character. Your fidelity is not to be extended frivolously. Unless you are quite confident about a person's character, you would do well to withhold your respect—both internally and externally. It is best to suspend judgment in such matters, unless and until it springs forth spontaneously.

9

The media are no more honest or reliable than are individual persons. The media are, after all, just aggregates of persons writing and speaking on behalf of this outlet, or that publication. Do not believe or accept any narrative merely because it appears in one or more "respected" sources. Much of the media are utterly undeserving of the reputations that they have accumulated over time. Newspapers are, in particular, far less reliable repositories of "news" than they are of partisan propaganda. A reputation for "objectivity" or "neutrality" is seldom deserved in this industry. Bias is almost inevitable. The same seems to be true, does it not, of individual persons? Objectivity and neutrality are not the default settings of the human condition.

10

Exercise your patience with children, animals, and imbeciles. Those who do not know any better can be (and should be) excused for their misbehavior. When it comes to those who are knowingly corrupt, however, you have no obligation to be particularly gentle or tolerant. Indeed, it is your obligation to expose acts and words that mislead, and the persons responsible for the attempted deception. Perhaps no one will heed your warning, or agree with your analysis, but you are responsible for offering honest assessments of duplicity when it is appropriate, and when you are competent to do so. Do not become arrogant or overly impressed with yourself, while exposing the skullduggery of others. You are often wrong—and you are no angel yourself.

Book XVII

1

If you receive praise, immediately pause to question its legit-imacy and the motive from which it issues. You must not believe yourself to be impressive merely because the idea appeals to you. Beware comforting beliefs. Do not accept any claim merely because you would be pleased if it were true. This includes claims about yourself. Only fools are swayed by flattery. You know (at least some of) your *many* flaws. Do not forget this. Anyone who fails to notice your peccadilloes is probably not paying attention—and probably for good reason.

2

To whom do you owe your commitment? Your family qualifies (with rare exceptions). Your nation, insofar as it behaves justly, has some claim upon you. Your Creator, assuming that there *is* a Creator, has an unassailable right to your reverence at all times, and your primary allegiance in all matters. With the exception of the Creator, all other alliances must be tempered by consider-ation of your duties as a rational agent. Blind faith is not a virtue in this spatiotemporal realm. If there is a God beyond this realm, you are to obey His commands—if you can discern them. Do your best. Do not expect perfection from yourself, but try to aim as close to perfect fidelity as you are able.

3

When people admire you or exhibit respect for you, remind yourself on every such occasion that this is a mere contingency, a happenstance, a result of events concatenated by forces you do not control. These are also, for the most part, people who do not know you very well, and who have not had to suffer for your inadequacies. Had your encounter occurred at a different place, a different time, under different circumstances, or with different people, it is quite likely that the assessment in question would have been turned on its head. Do not lightly convince yourself that the approval is deserved. Which of your accomplishments are so wonderful that they deserve any mention at all?

4

Make a study of your inclinations and proclivities. If you do not know your own mind and its tendencies, you are apt to fall into traps of your own making. Is your temper volatile? Moderate that tendency. Are you given to excessive drinking, eating, or pursuit of pleasure? Do not ignore this dysfunction within your character, but set your will to resisting too much indulgence. Be brutally honest about your shortcomings. Have someone remind you of these failings if necessary. Legend has it that a particular Emperor had an aide follow him through the square murmuring, "Remember, thou art mortal." The story is probably apocryphal, but its lesson is worth noting. This is a trust best reserved for someone of significant moral courage and fortitude.

5

Beware of sycophants. They seek to extract favors or some type of largesse. Be grateful for detractors. They seek to correct your behavior and keep you humble. Their motives may be malicious, but what business of yours is that? Ask yourself what motivates praise—especially when it is spoken out loud. Why not confine this high opinion of you or your abilities to the privacy of the speaker's mind? What is the additional benefit of the utterance? Is the praise offered in public, before a large crowd, or is it a private matter between just the two of you? This difference is not insignificant. To whom is the compliment intended to accrue, and to what end is it phrased just so? Manipulation is accomplished by interactions such as these. Is the praise meant *for* you, or only directed *at* you—with hope of winning your favor?

6

Are some moments and some experiences privileged relative to others? Are they "more real" or "deeper" than other elements of your life, and other experiences you may have? How so, exactly? Every moment is a component of the ensemble of events that you think of as "your" life (though you have never been quite clear in what sense it is "yours" exactly). Do not be swayed by intense pleasure, or heightened sensory stimulus, or novelty. This moment, right now, is neither more nor less a part of your life than is any other that you will ever experience. Indeed, right now is, in the final analysis, all you have. Yesterday has ceased to be. Do not ruminate on it. Tomorrow is not yet yours to experience, and there is no guarantee that it will be. Do not fantasize about it. Pay attention—now!

7

Let all childish fantasies of fame, fortune, power, and influence fade away along with the other intellectual detritus of youth. None of that is likely to be available to you in your real life, none of it is necessary for wisdom or virtue, and none of it would do you any good in any event. Indeed, you know yourself well enough to be fairly confident that fame would be toxic to you. Imagine people prying endlessly into your business, asking interminable questions, and imposing themselves upon you everywhere you go. There would be no peace for you in that style of life. You are made for being no one in particular.

8

Do not judge your progress by reference to other people. Some are far ahead of you, and some poor souls have not surpassed you yet. Keep the ideal of the sage always before your mind. Aim to develop the courage and fortitude of Socrates, Diogenes, the Stoics, the Spartan warriors, and Cato. To the extent that you fall short of this ideal, and you *will* fall short, you are to work that much more diligently than you have worked up to this point in your life. Never content yourself with any imagined superiority relative to the masses, or the average person, or the general run of humanity. Do not set the bar so low that you trip over it.

9

What is your primary duty, and where is it to be found? You have inviolate obligations. These supersede any and all competing considerations. These must, therefore, exist beyond the interference of external affairs and forces. Your most sacrosanct duties must be entirely up to you. What, then, is yours, and *only* yours, to control? What conditions are determined solely by your decision that things shall be thus and so? Can it be anything other than your will to ennoble your character? It cannot. What, then, contributes to the improvement of your character? These are the questions to which you must apply your limited powers of understanding and your intellect—mediocre though it is. Do not fritter away the little time and ability you have left. Narrow your focus, and concentrate your efforts. Cast off all that is inessential. Get to work.

10

No one promised you any benefits or pleasures from this life. Indeed, from the early texts, we are all told that this life is a "vale of tears," that suffering is the universal lot of all sentient beings, and that no one is spared. We are thrust into this without our consent. As is true of all before you, a tiny body emerged into the world, and almost immediately began stumbling, falling, and grasping blindly about. Moments of contentment, joy, or satisfaction, are more than you have any reason to expect—and you are *entitled* to *none* of them. Hang your head in shame if you find yourself bemoaning your fate, or complaining of circumstance. You have breathed the air, danced to music, seen mountains and oceans, and known the love of a good woman. If that is not enough for you, then you are a cantankerous toddler and a polyp upon the world. Do not complain of hardships and suffering. If it is too much for you, find a way out—but do so in shame. You have had it far easier than most.

Book XVIII

1

What is before your mind right now? Take notice of every subtlety, every facet, and every phenomenon. In what manner do thoughts and perceptions tend to arise? What mechanisms seem to connect them, one to another? How and when do they seem to pass away? You must know your mind's tendencies, if you are to have any hope of becoming its master. Do you perceive a "self" — a *perceiver* of the perceptions within your mind? Should you be troubled by the fact that you do not? How does one gain mastery, when one is not quite certain about the fundamental nature of one's self—if there *is* such a thing. *You* are thinking the matter through, are you not? This merits pause.

2

What kind of pathetic coward are you, that you cannot face the truth about yourself, your failings, and your poorly-lived life? An ostrich may hide its head for fear of what it may see. A human being does not have the excuse of only possessing a birdbrain. Weaklings lie to themselves, and others, about their character and their abilities, because they are desperate to appear strong and courageous. Are you content to be *both* a weakling and a coward? Where, precisely, is one to look for evidence indicating the contrary? If you are not content, then you are free to refuse to abase yourself further. You are free to do something about yourself. Be an adult, or be done with the charade. Do not be a waste of your own time.

3

The world cannot break you. It cannot demoralize you. It cannot force you to give up. It cannot compel you to indignity. The world has no purchase on any of that. It can, and it will, *kill* you. Can it, though, force you to *fear* death, and go whimpering to it? Try to enjoy death when the moment arrives. What is there to lose—but your fear? Time will erode away your strength and vitality, or a sudden turn of events may snatch your last breath without warning. This is not up to you. A broken spirit, a broken will, can only be the product of your surrender. Decide, right now, that you shall *never* surrender in this manner. Make yourself impervious to the temptation. Μολὼν λαβέ!

4

Do nothing half-heartedly. A task worth time and energy is a task worthy of your full attention. When you find your mind drifting away from the task at hand, either command its return and sharpen your focus, or lay the matter before you aside, and follow your attention's drift with intellectual vigor. Perhaps your subconscious has noted something important of which you are not yet aware. Seek the value, if there is any to be had, in this shift of your attention. Perhaps your conscious mind has missed something that some other element of your psyche perceives, and in which it has legitimate interest. Of course, you may just need a nap.

5

What is this obsession with celebrity? It afflicts not only contemporary culture, but *you* have also allowed yourself to be caught up in it from time to time. Who are these "luminaries" that anyone should concern themselves with the comings and goings of actors, singers, or performers of other trivial tricks? If you find yourself sliding, yet again, into this cultural pathology, snap yourself immediately, and brutally, back to sanity. Literally slap yourself if necessary. Do not trifle with such nonsense. There is work to be done.

6

War, economic collapse, and chaos seem to threaten everywhere around the globe. It seems that some terrorist attack or other occurs every week—sometimes it is several *per* week. Mass migration seems almost designed to make life unlivable for the native inhabitants of the nations on the receiving end. No culture can absorb the unassimilable in their millions, and remain what it once had been. Yes, but what is all of that to you? Can you forestall any of this by the sheer force of your will? If so, get to it! If not, why allow yourself to be distracted from the task of self-rectification? Society will either fly apart, or it will not. Take notice of events, prepare for a future without law, order, or easy access to necessities—and then get back to the real work. Attend to material affairs so that you can turn your attention back inward where it belongs. Do not weep for your dying society. It was never built to last.

7

Do your best to learn the most effective methods, and to master the most reliable weapons, to be deployed in defense of your family, yourself, and innocents under your care. It is not permissible to leave this responsibility to anyone else, or any government agency. The police will arrive in time to scrape your carcass off of the pavement. They are not really designed for the prevention of violent crime. You never know where or when the critical situation may arise. Be always prepared to become protector and defender—in less than the blink of an eye. Become brutality incarnate if necessary. Do not deny this element of your nature. You have always been aware of what smolders beneath your façade of civility. The matter is not for public consumption, but you must be able to access the bestial element within you, should the moment present itself. Control it, but do not hesitate to let slip the savage if the time comes. He will, unfortunately, prove a handy fellow.

8

Limit your dependencies as much as you are able. Basic food, water, and shelter have always been necessities, and they can all be had outside of the typical methods and avenues of procurement. Beyond these material basics, you must try to take matters of health and psychological stability into your own hands, and be responsible for your own rigorous discipline. You have long suspected that daily rituals of civility and reflexive dependence upon modern conveniences has made you softer than you ought to be. You also know that you carry a vestigial dysfunction in your head. The well-functioning limbic system seems not to have made its way fully into your ancestry. Descended from lizards, you are. Medications may be necessary, for the time being, but their future availability cannot be assured. Should a disruption of distribution systems occur, you must be prepared to proceed without pharmaceutical assistance. You must develop means of psychological sustenance that will remain readily available, come what may. Cultivate mental rectitude. There *are* methods.

9

If you have the capacity to accomplish something on your own, then a request for help is an admission of either weakness, sloth, or indifference. An exception might be made for the sake of efficiency. Many hands can, indeed, make the work lighter and speed completion of the task. For the inner work, however, look first to your *own* efforts. Consult the sages as frequently as you require, but recognize that their words must be implemented through *your* efforts. The Buddha is not going to solve your problems with a "laying on of hands," and Diogenes is not here to spit in your face and wake you up. No, self-discipline is, ultimately, an activity of the self. Help is *not* on the way.

10

If your neighbor chooses a dissolute life, this is none of your business. Your neighbor's life was never delivered into your hands. Let him be. If, however, the neighbor's lifestyle begins to encroach upon your family's safety or good health, then address the issue swiftly and unambiguously. Be utterly clear about your concerns, and about the proposed remedy. Half measures will only stave off the inevitable for a short while (if that). Make it clear that you are both willing and able to rip out the threat, roots and all, if it must come to that. If this means the deterioration of good neighborly relations, so be it. You have nothing to gain through association with those who cannot be counted on to at least *attempt* neighborly decency. Never allow the miscreant to rule your home turf.

Book XIX

1

Suppose that there is no God, that there are no souls, that there is no design plan for this universe, and that we are ultimately "consigned to oblivion," both as individuals and collectively. We are doomed. What of it? You still have before you the choice of reason and decency, or unguided appetite and degeneracy. You can live nobly or ignobly—even if nothing further follows. What is the benefit of a life led by anything other than reason? What is the point of pursuits that have no connection with wisdom? It is better to emulate Socrates than a pig, no matter what the surrounding circumstances may be. Perhaps we live in a vast, cosmological sty. Fine. A Socrates covered in filth is still preferable to a swine feeding at the trough.

2

Mind your appetites. Nothing will cause you more trouble and weaken your will more quickly and more thoroughly than unchecked, selfish desire (especially if it is of unwholesome origin). Pleasures of the flesh are not problematic in and of themselves, but they open a door to foul misdeeds if passion is left ungoverned by reason. Your desire has a proper object, and hosts of utterly improper potential objects. Direct it wisely. Prize virtue more highly than bestial impulses directed at short-term gratification. Resist the darkest temptations. Do not subordinate honor to base impulse. You are *not*, in fact, a pig.

3

A lie told in a moment of panic is no less deceitful than a premeditated prevarication. Both violate your obligation to be honest with others, as well as with yourself. You are not excused from this obligation merely because you have been caught off guard. If you cannot tell the truth on a moment's notice, do not think yourself honest or trustworthy, and do not tell others that they may safely place their confidence in you. If you lie as a reflex, then your honesty can only be calculated. What kind of "honesty" is that?

4

Your temper has gotten the better of you once again, has it not? Imbecile! Ape! It makes no difference that you were provoked by a liar, or by a corrupt cheat, or by a pompous windbag. The failure is *yours*—again! Their indifference to decency and honor does not liberate you to lower yourself in a flash of virulent, irrational anger. Are you not adult enough to endure the misdeeds of your fellow human beings? If not, you are a weakling, and you ought to dispense with all pretense of pursuing wisdom and self-control. What is it that you claim to be? What do you tell yourself you strive to achieve? Do you aim to become the equivalent of an irascible baboon? Grow up, you simian reprobate. A rational adult is not hurled into a tizzy by mere words and gestures. What concern is it of yours if someone makes these sounds, or those movements of the hands? Mind your business.

5

Mind your own affairs, thickhead. Do not get caught up in concern over what other people are doing, thinking, feeling, and saying. They are autonomous beings (more or less), and their behavior is none of your concern. Their lives and their comings and goings have not been entrusted to you. If someone *requests* your input, offer the most thoughtful, and hopefully, helpful response you can muster. Do not, however, impose your yammering upon those who have not asked your opinion. Who died and made you consigliere?

6

Intellectual humility is essential to growth and learning. If you convince yourself that you already know all there is to be learned about any particular subject, this stultifies further inquiry and reflection. Socrates understood and embraced his ignorance in order that he might *pursue* wisdom and virtue. Those who erroneously thought themselves wise were subjected to his rigorous questioning and skeptical analysis. Few withstood the challenge. Do not allow overconfidence to stand athwart inquiry and edification. You begin to learn only when you recognize the need to improve yourself and your understanding of the world in which you find yourself embedded. You begin to learn when you realize that you *need* to learn. Have you, therefore, even *begun* the project?

7

Those who declare themselves experts should be treated to a healthy dose of rational skepticism. You should neither accept nor reject what they say merely because they say it. Anyone can, after all, *say* anything. Do not be impressed with titles, degrees, or reputation. You have known too many educated imbeciles to take such flotsam as indicative of genuine wisdom or understanding. Investigate every claim as thoroughly as the subject matter warrants. Carry the inquiry as far as you are able. You have no excuse for failing to think for *yourself*. Do not say, "But someone else has been kind enough to do the thinking for me." *That* is a preamble to serfdom.

8

Avoid being presumptuous. It is unwise to assume that you know the contents of another person's mind merely because of a few comments or a few actions. What do other people think that they know about *you*? Based on what you say and do, the picture *cannot* be flattering. Remember that motivations are not immediately available to your perception, and remember also that specific behaviors sometimes diverge from one's general cast of character. Everyone has an "off day" now and again. Words spoken in anger or frustration may not indicate a more general tendency or inclination of character. Perfect consistency is rare. Perhaps it is so rare that it has never actually been enacted by a member of your primate species. Even Jesus lost his temper with the moneychangers. This does not mean that perfect consistency cannot function as a regulative *ideal*. Let it be *your* goal. Do not *demand* it of others. Do not *expect* it of yourself. There is, however, something pleasant about the thought of it, is there not?

9

A playful moment is nothing of which you ought to feel ashamed. There is nothing so terrible about a bit of frivolity, a good belly laugh, or a brief respite from severity and discipline—provided, of course, that the respite does not undercut or impede your overall progress. Do not, however, allow silliness to become a *habit*. The frivolous should not become a hallmark of your character. If you wish to live as a clown, there are still circuses that may take you in. If you wish to walk in the steps of Socrates, Diogenes, Seneca, Epictetus, and Marcus Aurelius, then you have no time for face paint or a rubber nose. The real work must come *first* with you.

10

Arrange your material affairs—your finances, security, and such—so that they may be dealt with in swift, efficient fashion. You should be able to turn to such concerns only briefly, without a great deal of rigmarole, and readily rectify any deficiencies or discrepancies regarding your fiscal stability. These concerns are not the center of your style of life, your overarching values, or your primary project. Certain basic material conditions must be satisfied if you are to accomplish anything else. Starving or dying of a virus is hardly a reliable methodology of enhancing mental discipline. Having satisfied the basic conditions of continued existence, turn your attention back to the work that is your true purpose. Do not dwell too long over surface practicalities. Once the wood has been chopped, and the water carried, you must turn your attention back to your will and its proper direction. The external world has a way of seizing control of the internal, if you allow it.

Book XX

1

Thoughts and actions are not quite the separate spheres of phenomena that many take them to be. It is very rare to find anyone whose thoughts and actions diverge sharply or thoroughly from one another. If you think a great deal about money, for example, it is difficult to avoid either miserliness or prodigality. Similarly, if you spend a great deal of time working on physical fitness and your appearance, it is difficult to avoid an unhealthy narcissism, or some type of dysmorphic disorder. Thoughts and deeds inform one another. They shape one another to some degree. Your mind must, therefore, be turned as often as possible to the improvement of your character and the attainment of virtue and wisdom. If these are not the primary objects of your consideration, they are unlikely to be the primary areas in which you make progress.

2

Unsolicited advice is generally unbecoming and usually unwelcome. Who are you that you believe yourself entitled to shove your opinions into another adult's face and mind? Children may require frequent correction and guidance, even when it is unbidden. Not everyone, however, is a child. Certainly, not everyone is *your* child or your responsibility. Do your best to offer sound advice when *asked* for it. Otherwise, let people live their own lives. You tend to *yours*. Do you not find enough of your own shortcomings to keep you busy?

3

You will not be here for long. Even if you live one hundred years, your presence on this planet is less than the blink of a cosmological eye. Once you are gone, you will be remembered neither long nor by many. This is as it should be, is it not? You are an ephemeral life form among untold billions of others. Those that lived before you are gone, and you have taken notice of *very* few of them. Posterity will pay you no more mind than you have paid the "commoners" who have gone before you. Future persons would be foolish to waste their limited time attending to the stray mutterings and musing of some talking ape with shoes. You will be a corpse, and then you will be dust. Is that so much to ask?

4

The thing about the inevitable is that there is just no getting around it. Do not delude yourself about what is coming. All you can foresee, of course, is but a miniscule fragment of all that shall come to pass—but what you can foresee is not *nothing* either, and it is not illusory. You know how *your* story ends. You know not when, where, or how, but you know the "way of all flesh," and you can see and feel that you are, in fact, composed of flesh— your body is, at any rate. If there is a soul, you have not seen it. Get to work on doing the best that you can in all matters worthy of your time and effort. You have *much* work to do. The hour begins to feel late, does it not?

5

What do you care about anyone's opinion—including your own? If new evidence prevails, will you not change your mind? You must follow the evidence wherever it may lead. If not, you are a sad excuse for a "rational animal," and of relatively little use to the world, your fellow "rational animals," or yourself. Opinions come and go as quickly as the water rushes down the riverbed. Only a fool clings to darling opinions against the force of reason and evidence. Are you a fool? The question is sincere.

6

Do not pretend to respect persons for whom you have developed a legitimate contempt—keeping in mind that you can never be quite certain about the legitimacy of your contempt. Remain open to the possibility that your assessment is a function of some failing of *yours,* or some misinterpretation of events, but do not succumb to the all too common tendency to irrational and unjustifiable charity in such matters. Taking people "at their word" is foolhardy and contrary to most of the available evidence about the degree of honesty to be found among the masses. People lie. People are full of pretense and charade. People misrepresent themselves at least as easily as they tell true tales of their character and their real interests. They are not to be trusted by default. They are not to be trusted without having *earned* that trust. By the way, *you* are a person. Are you or are you not to be trusted? Another sincere question.

7

Once again, your temper has gotten the better of you, has it not? You are like a shrew combined with a snake. What excuse are you prepared to offer this time? Someone made a derogatory comment about you? Oh, poor baby. Someone made noise with a face other than your own. Is this "too much" for you? Their words are none of your business. Everyone is free to speak as they wish. If they choose to disparage you, how does this justify an outburst of emotion? There is nothing sacrosanct about you. You are *not* special! Your name, your reputation, and your (overly delicate) sensibilities are irrational objects of concern. Can you not bear up under the onslaught of words? Weakling. Taking "offense" (whatever that means) is just another form of feebleness. Go soak your head.

8

Have you lost some money or gotten a "raw deal" in the marketplace? It happens. This story is not novel in any way. Lots of people get "ripped off," do they not? You do not get to keep the money *forever* in any event. When you drop dead (which will not be so very long from now), the money remains behind. Is dying with a few dollars less to your name some kind of tragedy for which your peace of mind is rightly sacrificed? If your serenity can be dispelled by the loss of a bit of money, then your mind is just another commodity. You have turned yourself into the psychological equivalent of a prostitute. Proud of that, are you? Do *not* sell yourself. There is a word for persons in *that* profession. It is less pleasant than "prostitute."

9

You must exercise your mind and your will far, *far* more often, and more carefully, than you exercise your body. How much damage has your body sustained due to training mishaps, collisions, and general wear and tear? Is it not likely that faulty intellectual "gymnastics" are at least as dangerous to you? When you deploy your mind less than artfully, you set yourself up for damages incurred, and the long-term consequences thereof. Atrophy, by the way, is another unfortunate condition worth avoiding. This can be accomplished only through diligent exertion and hard work. So, get to work.

10

How little you understand about God. Indeed, you do not *know* for certain that a Creator or Designer actually *exists*. If there *is* a God, you have relatively little idea of what scripture, if any, is closest to an accurate description of the Deity, or a reliable account of divine dictates. Is there not something a bit unsettling about this? Your ignorance ought to trouble you a bit. After all, if there is a Creator, you only exist because the Creator has provided a world for you, and for everyone else. Perhaps you have not devoted the requisite attention to this matter. What is your excuse for this lassitude? You are frightened, are you not? You are terrified that there is a God who disapproves of you or your life, and you are terrified that there is no God, and you are the product of a series of accidents, or of mere evolutionary happenstance. Why does this latter possibility engender in you the feeling that you are, somehow, a reptile? Is it something about being cold-blooded that asserts itself? This is confusing business. You want God to be real. That, of course, does not make it so— but do not deny this aspect of your character.

Book XXI

1

Patience is, indeed, a virtue—for the most part. It is, however, relatively useless without tenacity, courage, and industriousness. Without these, patience is largely a matter of waiting hopefully. Your dog can do that. You will not attain wisdom by waiting and hoping that it may spontaneously arise of its own accord. There *are*, after all, *old* fools. You have met more of them than you would have imagined a few years ago. Take care that you do not become one of them.

2

God bless the fighters! The peacemakers have their place as well, of course, but the fighters lay their lives and bodies on the line and, at least sometimes, they do so for their beliefs, values, and convictions. You cannot help but respect courage of that magnitude, even if it resides in an opponent's camp, or is deployed by an enemy that you find despicable, or if it rears its head in a contest that you regard as unwise or indefensible. Active virtue is not properly disdained. Acts of courage are intrinsically noble. Even the unjust can exhibit flashes of nobility. Even your enemy can inspire your admiration. Can *you*?

3

Human life is either intrinsically valuable, or it is not. If human life is worthy of preservation, it clearly makes no difference whether that life is developing within the womb, or learning to crawl. A "fetus" travels about three feet and becomes an "infant"? Is this alteration morally significant? How so? A human future is valuable, or it is not. If you value *your* future, you are a hypocrite if you do not recognize and defend the value of the unborn. Were you not unborn once yourself? Are you not grateful for the opportunity you have had to draw breath—and all that followed after? A woman's womb is not an abattoir. You struggle to understand the cavalier attitude so often exhibited toward the most defenseless and innocent human beings among us. The unborn *are* human, and they *are* beings. Check the genetics. Note the continuum from zygote to adult human being. Do you find a sharp break anywhere? Do you understand those who claim this crucial moral threshold? Perhaps that particular struggle is unworthy of quite so much effort. Whence the obligation to understand depravity? Abortion is the moral equivalent of murder. Do not pretend that you do not understand this.

4

There is nothing wrong with competition, provided that you do not become emotionally invested in "victory" or psychologically averse to "defeat." Winning and losing are not entirely within your control. Your opponent is competing as hard as you are, and no one is invincible. Thus, the real competition, the part that you can control, is the exertion of the best effort that you can muster on the occasion in question, given the prevailing circumstances. Your role is to do your best. Having done so, pay no mind to the outcome. If you fail to do the best that you are able, analyze the reasons for this. What caused you to exert less than your finest effort on this occasion? Is the problem a weakness in your character, is it a contingent circumstance, or is it something else entirely? Correct any deficiencies in yourself that you may find, and return to compete again. Focus on your performance and the preparations in which you engage. Winning and losing are beside the point.

5

Beware the potential for decision paralysis. When faced with time constraints, *no* decision is, in all too many circumstances, worse than a bad decision. Inaction is seldom conducive to efficacy as a rational agent. Reason as best you can, given the limitations you face, and translate efficient deliberations into decisive actions. Do not hesitate due to fear. Do not boggle at a vast diversity of options. The most fundamental guiding principles to which you adhere should be sufficiently clear, and broadly applicable, so that many potential options can be quickly eliminated from consideration. Nothing inappropriate or dishonest should even come to mind, and any such consideration must be immediately dismissed. Decency is usually a fairly narrow path. Ignore any options that diverge from the path of decency and righteousness.

6

You have been insufficiently grateful for the many unearned benefits that you have been granted. How often have you considered the time, place, and conditions of your birth? How many times have you consciously given thanks for a body and mind that function within normal parameters (for the most part)? Have you fully appreciated your family, your nation, your culture, your opportunities, and your material comforts? None of these are *necessary* for you to live a life in accordance with reason and dignity, but the presence of these advantages is, for practical purposes, overwhelmingly preferable to their absence. Consider the lot of all those who have been granted none of these advantages you enjoy, and remind yourself frequently that you could have been one of those persons. Gratitude must never be far from your mind.

7

You need not alter your appearance to please anyone. Thoreau cautioned against endeavors that require new clothes. There is wisdom in this counsel. Why are your old clothes deficient for some new association or experience? Who are these people who require your apparel to meet their standards, and what has clothing got to do with decency and honor? A well-dressed malefactor is not more tolerable because he wears an expensive suit. A wise man dressed in rags (and have not most of the wisest men eschewed concern for such matters?) is not less worthy of your respect because he does not wear a necktie and newly shined shoes. A pretty face does not make a woman any more worthy of your trust. An athlete is not a better human being for possessing greater physical gifts than the norm. Attend to your character. Try to be an Olympian of virtue. Leave appearances to actors and politicians.

8

Your wife, your spouse, your most important friend and associate as the two of you move through this life, is to be treated with respect and kindness at *all* times, and in *all* matters. Hang your head in shame if you ever so much as entertain any form of malice toward her, or disinterest in her welfare. You are *not* a man if you mistreat your wife in any way. Should you do so, she would be justified in destroying you in your sleep. Adult males who abuse their wives are "men" in name only. They have earned your contempt, the disapprobation of the masses, and they deserve to suffer for their repugnant behavior. This vile behavior is *not* to be tolerated. You will not "look the other way" if you become aware of this type of conduct. Do not falter here.

9

If your will is *not* free, whom do you blame for this? How is causal determinism an affront? If heredity and environment determine your will, then your will is in harmony with nature. Your ancestors cannot have been other than they were. The laws of nature are either up to no one, or they are God's handiwork. There is either design underpinning the universe, or the cosmos unfolds without guidance of any kind. Do you trust God's will and judgment less than your own? If there is not a God, and the brute forces of nature are, in fact, unguided, do you set yourself up in opposition to the natural realm? Good luck with your opposition to the universe. If, on the other hand, your will *is* actually free, then use it! Take control of yourself, learn what you must, and govern your life like an adult. Blame no one. Do not be petulant.

10

You have no business wanting anything that you do not have— with the exception of wisdom. As for the material world, you disgrace yourself if you covet anything that you do not possess. How weak and needy are you that you allow yourself to suffer for want of some trinket, or some greater amount of money than you possess, or some unnecessary luxury that can be purchased at some price or other? How ungrateful is this insistence upon having more than you have been granted? All that you truly need has been afforded to you in abundance. You should be embarrassed to want more than you have. You should be still more embarrassed to fail to appreciate all that for which you do *not* want, and all that you have been granted without earning any of it. If you cannot *will* it, you have no business *wanting* it. You should *want* your will to adhere to the dictates of reason. The moment you begin to blame anyone or anything other than yourself for your weakness and inadequacy, you thereby expose yourself as a blight on the planet. Stop your whining and get to work.

Book XXII

1

When a charlatan cons an imbecile out of a sum of money, where do you place the blame? The imbecile probably cannot help the intellectual deficiency on display. Stupidity has eluded any cure—and not for lack of searching. The charlatan probably cannot resist the impulse to take advantage of the stupid. Perhaps this is a natural inclination, with some degree of evolutionary advantage. This is not impossible. Perhaps early childhood development, or some trauma, has induced a coping mechanism that manifests in the interrelations at issue. In the final analysis, it may be that some people just are, so to speak, "wolves," and others are just "sheep." Is it wrong for wolves to feed upon sheep? If so, what is a wolf to do?

2

When the truth needs to be told, and you are reasonably confident that you know the truth, and that you can provide the relevant evidence and argument, you *must* speak the truth—especially when the truth is troubling or unpopular. If you have any obligations pertaining to speech acts, surely this is one. Part of your role is to be the teller of uncomfortable truths. You will be criticized, your words will be rejected, and you may well be ostracized. You are to speak the truth nonetheless. Do not desert your post. If you must suffer "slings and arrows" as you stand your post, then suffer them. What is this to you? Will you make of yourself a coward and a liar to appease others? Whose opinion of you is worth this debasement of self, soul, and character? Stand your post.

3

You have no obligation to laugh merely for the sake of conviviality. Civility is, generally, a virtue. It is not appropriate, however, to encourage attempts at humor that are either inappropriate or simply not funny. A "charitable" chuckle is a bit of condescension, and it is patronizing. The impulse to be charitable or sociable can be difficult to resist. Being the only person not participating in a standing ovation is apt to be uncomfortable. This is due to a failure to discipline your mind and your emotions, is it not? Your level of comfort should not be impacted by the disapprobation of friends, colleagues, or strangers. Let them agree amongst themselves. Let them laugh and applaud together. You need not join in, and you certainly need not concern yourself about what other persons believe. A noble silence sometimes speaks loudly.

4

You are either your own person, or you are no individual at all. There is no such thing as being someone else's person. Adhering to someone else's dictates is voluntary servitude. Are you a herd animal? Are you a dog running with the pack? If so, then get down on all fours and stop pretending that you are an autonomous, rational being. You are possessed of a capacity that was once referred to as "a spark of the divine." Whether it is that, or just a coincident of some evolutionary adaptation, your reason is to be marshaled in pursuit of truth, wisdom, and virtue. If you are not busy about *that* project, what is the object of your efforts? To waste your limited resources on all too common trivialities is nothing admirable. You ennoble yourself, or you fail to ennoble yourself. The choice is yours.

5

The temptation to make idols of human constructs is to be conscientiously avoided. Misplaced reverence for the imperfect works of talking apes has led to some of the most atrocious conduct ever to have beset and befallen humanity or, indeed, animal life on the planet. Sociopolitical ideology is less than divine in any and all of its manifestations. Manifestos and brickbats are not exactly carved into stone by the inerrant finger of the Lord. Men construct systems of belief and have a tendency to fall in love with their theories. Be careful about pledging your allegiance to scribblers and bureaucrats. You need not join a movement to improve yourself. You are not, at heart, a "joiner." Turn your attention inward when you hear a crowd chanting slogans or singing anthems. Do not be seduced by a cacophony of roused voices.

6

The only real laws that you will ever encounter are laws of nature. Civil "laws" are regularly broken, violated, ignored, and can be altered on a passing whim. The term "law" is misleading in this arena. You are free to disregard civil dictates, and to embrace the possible consequences of doing so. Never tell yourself that you are *compelled* to do thus-and-so, or that you are *prevented* from doing this or that, merely because the law prescribes the former and proscribes the latter. This is an excuse. If you think it both right and reasonable to violate a law of the land, and if you are willing to face possible sanction for doing so, then "screw your courage to the sticking place," steel your spine, and act. Do not supplicate yourself before a piece of legislation or imaginary constraints.

7

Are you angry and frustrated by corruption? Why? Unless *you* have fallen into the practice of corruption, why is this matter of any significance to you? Surely, it cannot still surprise you that so many of your fellow human beings value decency less than they value money and power. How many times can you encounter any phenomenon and still allow yourself to be shocked by it? If you are not the corrupt individual in the instance in question, then your anger and frustration are directed against states of affairs concerning which your will has no purchase. Your psychological and emotional states are not relevant to the matter at issue. Does your anger help solve the problem? Does it do you, or anyone else, any good? Is it a purgative? Speak out if you believe that doing so will call attention to the injustice. Doing so in a state of rage is hardly likely to be helpful though, is it? If anything, your ire will unbalance you and undermine your message. Reason is more useful than rage. You *know* this.

8

Nothing good ensues from denying your nature. This does not, of course, mean that you passively accept your flaws, or that you stop working on self-improvement. That would be foolishness and a waste of life. Do not, however, attempt to be, as it were, "taller than you are," or more talented in some area than your physiology allows. You are not, and never will be, an Einstein, or a Shakespeare, or a Picasso. You are not endowed with the requisite gifts of nature. Fortunately, neither nature nor virtue demands of you anything that is beyond your capacities. You cannot be required to do anything that is, for you, impossible. Your duty is to do the best that you can. Now, set about doing your duty.

9

Your pets are a great advantage to you, and you ought to treasure them. Few human beings are capable of the unadulterated affection, or the spontaneous joy with which your dog greets you every morning, and every time you return home. There is no guile in your dog. There is no need to be concerned about ulterior motives or hidden agendas. Your cat, while not nearly as affectionate, is a model of simplicity in rest, and shares extended periods of serene repose with you. Your lap is warm, so he places himself there. It could not be simpler. A cat asleep on your lap or your chest provides a calming influence nearly unrivaled among your human companions. Animals impose relatively little by way of expectations, dispute, or droning vapidity. Sleep, food, play, and companionship are on offer at minimal cost. With occasional exceptions, this is a very felicitous bargain.

10

Ambiguity is not entirely avoidable, but it is not to be trusted. Often, ambiguous statements are intended to obfuscate, conceal, and provide cover for subsequent denials, reversals, or evasions. Clarity and precision are virtues in nearly all forms of communication. No one speaks or writes with double meanings in an attempt to reveal the truth—unless the subject matter *itself* is inherently ill-defined or ineffable. You must develop the capacity to identify and note unnecessary ambiguity in expression. It should give you pause regarding the speaker's intentions, as well as the potential import of the concealment at issue. What is it that you are intended *not* to understand? Why the cunning maneuver, and to whom derives the benefit? Stop and consider the reason for any semantic contortionism you encounter. Honesty is rarely the motivation for needlessly abstruse expression. Why "abstruse"? Can you not help yourself even *now*?

Book XXIII

1

Remember that aging is not punishment, neither is it something to lament. You have heard it said that it is "better than the alternative," but this seems to be less than *necessarily* the case. Some lives are, at least arguably, not worth living. For *you*, for *now*, aging *is* preferable to the alternative. Do not, therefore, complain about the aches, pains, diminished physical capacities, or any of the rest that goes along with *not dropping dead*. More importantly, be grateful for the extension of time and opportunity to pursue wisdom and virtue. Every moment spent grumbling about your back, your knees, or your digestive tract, is an opportunity wasted. Every moment not spent improving your character is a moment of stagnation or decline.

2

You do not know when the end is coming for anyone. Death comes when it will, not only when it is welcomed or when it is "time." There is, in fact, no such thing as dying "before one's time," any more than there is such a thing as being born "before one's time." If you die tomorrow, you will have been cheated out of *nothing*. No guarantees were issued to you, no promises were made, and you did not *earn* your way into this life. If providence placed you here, then you serve "at the Master's will," and if you are nothing more than a chance concurrence of antecedent conditions and laws of nature, then you can lay claim to no fixed span of life. If there is no Designer, then the whole thing is a crapshoot. In any event, you do not get a vote in this matter.

3

If you find that you are disappointed with anyone, ask yourself how many times you have disappointed others—to say nothing of the many occasions that you have fallen short by your own lights. Can you justify sustained anger or resentment directed at someone who is guilty of the kinds of transgressions that you have committed more times than you care to count? Do not allow any degree of (alleged) self-improvement to convince you that you are now authorized to regard yourself as superior to anyone else. Were you not once very much the same as those you now behold? Is it a certainty that you will not, one day, become *again* as they are now? It would not, after all, be your first experience of backsliding. Do not become overly impressed with yourself. No one else is.

4

Remember that the first lie generally leads to others—sometimes it leads to *many* others. You must often tell subsequent lies to cover the initial deception. Each new prevarication carries with it the possibility of exposure. The consequences are potentially limitless, and the anxiety over being discovered expands and metastasizes with each new untruth, and every new pair of eyes and ears investigating the matter. This is just part of the "tangled web we weave," when we render ourselves false, and Shakespeare was quite correct about the "practice" of deception. All of it is entirely needless. There are no conditions *requiring* deceit. It is always possible to tell the truth. You only need to develop the fortitude to do so.

5

If you are perturbed when people and bureaucracies waste your time, why do you so relentlessly fritter away so much of your time and energy on nonsense, vapid entertainments, and trivial concerns? You inflict upon yourself far greater losses in this arena than have ever been squandered standing in line, filling out forms, or jumping through hoops. How much mindless television have you consumed thus far? How many hours have you lain in bed, after the sleeping is done, but before the work has begun? This is nothing more than procrastination and sloth. How many times have you listened to the same song, or indulged in the same pointless ritual or routine? No one can waste more of your life than *you*. Yet, you grumble about a "waste of your time"? Hypocrite.

6

From what source does your discontent arise today? Is someone making unjustified demands on your time and attention? Let the matter be known and walk away. Is this not within your power? Doing so might jeopardize your job or some relationship with a friend or colleague. So? What is of greater value? If the job is more important than the irritant, put the irritation out of your mind, focus on the task at hand like an adult, and complete matters efficiently, so as to be more quickly freed to go about your business. If the job is not sufficiently important to warrant the imposition, leave the job behind, as well as the burden on your time and energy, then go about doing as you wish. Either way, your contentment is in *your* hands. Griping is a poor substitute for *doing*.

7

How long do you plan to maintain the charade of sharing values and interests with those who occupy a worldview utterly alien to you? If you have no interest in the "great questions of the day," stop participating in tedious discussion and debate on these topics. Is someone fascinated by the performance of the stock markets, or the probable outcome of some sporting event? Leave that person and that interest be. What is any of it to you? There is no need to join in the blathering back and forth about such silliness, and there is no point in feigning interest merely to placate a colleague or a friend. No one needs you to share their every fascination. Why this compulsion to pretend that you care about such matters? It is perfectly permissible to shrug and turn away. Even if others do *not* deem it permissible, nothing *prevents* you from doing as you wish.

8

Tomorrow may require all the resolve that you can muster, and all that you can muster may well prove to be insufficient to the challenge at hand. You may not have the power or the resources to bring events into line with hopes or expectations. You are *not*, for that reason, excused from exerting every possible ounce of effort and iota of will at your disposal. You will give everything you have, you will spend yourself to exhaustion if need be, and you will drop before you relent. Should your efforts prove inadequate to the test, let it be so because of the magnitude of the venture, and not due to the paucity of your efforts. There is no shame in not planting your flag at the summit. If you do not make it there because you did not really try, however, you would have done better to stay in bed. Decide in advance that you will allow your body to break before you allow your spirit to do so.

9

Do not expect to encounter justice, fair play, or objectivity in significant quantities today. They are not found frequently, and they are generally more than counterbalanced by corruption, fraud, and partisanship. It is not your role to complain about how unfair the world is, or about dirty dealing among politicians, captains of industry, or even among drunks at the corner pub. Your role is to be an example, even if only a small and mostly unnoticed one, of decency and honor. Frankly, you are not serving that role nearly as effectively or as consistently as you should. Do not caterwaul about the failings of the powerful when you do not even manage your own affairs virtuously. *Your* behavior is your business.

10

What is Independence Day to you? The nation may celebrate, but a nation is something of an abstraction, is it not? From what, or from whom, do *you* declare your independence? Are you subject to no empire? Do not delude yourself. How often have you taken off in a direction prohibited by the state, or by social custom, or by general expectation? You can count such adventures on the fingers of *one* hand—and yet you fantasize almost daily about casting off the bonds of conventionality. You dream, but you do not act—and *that* is the mark of a coward. Epictetus said, "No man is free who is not master of himself." By this standard, you are *far* from free. Epictetus was born a slave, he was crippled by repeated torture, and yet he enjoyed greater independence than you have ever known.

Book XXIV

1

Do you sometimes fancy yourself sturdily built in both body and mind? If so, stop to consider all those you have known, all those you have seen, and all those about whom you have read, to whom you could not hold a candle in either respect. Are you sturdier of mind than was the Buddha? Are you physically superior to contemporary Olympians, or the Spartans of ancient Greece? Does your constancy of purpose surpass that of Socrates, Diogenes, Epictetus, or Marcus Aurelius? In all of these cases, and in innumerably more, you are as a child by comparison. Do not fall into the bad habit of comparing yourself to the modern day herd. Aim higher than that or give up altogether. You begin to wonder if you really are more wolf than sheep. This is not a good sign. Wolves show no indication of similar self-doubt.

2

Poe referred to the "Imp of the Perverse," and claimed that its compulsion is as captivating as the call of virtue, decency, and even self-preservation. Have you not felt this Imp's call at times? Have you not contemplated stepping out into the void off of a mountain ridge path, or steering into oncoming traffic, or calling out obscenities at some somber ritual? You should take no pride in any of that, but you must admit to having these experiences. What is this strange urge to do what ought not to be done, to imperil yourself needlessly, or to harm the innocent for no reason other than the illogic and willfulness of doing so? Poe was attuned to something. *Never* weaken and accede to the Imp of the Perverse. Nothing wholesome shall ensue.

3

Savagery must often be met with greater and more acute

savagery. Do not turn away from cases of bestial carnage in horror, despair, or indifference. It may well be true that violence tends to lead to more violence, but the object of the violence is *not* irrelevant in such considerations. The savagery of genocide is not properly met with diplomacy, tact, or forbearance. Time is of the essence, the lives of innocents hang in the balance, and you are not excused from defending the defenseless merely because that act of protection requires bloodshed. When blood is already being spilled, and more is forthcoming, do not kid yourself that all butchery is equal. Killing terrorists is *not* evil. They have jettisoned their humanity, and removed themselves from what Kant called "the kingdom of ends." They are mere things, masquerading as persons. Pitiless brutality is their lot.

4

What threat are you unable to face with courage, reason, and fortitude? A knife to your throat is not an endangerment to your honor. You need not buckle and abase yourself because of a blade. Will you be deprived of life if you refuse to obey? Perhaps you will. Indeed, that result is probable. So be it! Where did you get the idea that you are otherwise immortal? Death is coming for you anyway. Is it not preferable to expire with your decency intact, than to persist as a coward, a weakling, or a pathetic wretch tainted with ignominy and the disingenuous excuse of duress? Look death right in the eye. Give it a playful wink. Offer your carotid artery and your jugular, but never offer up your soul. No one can deprive you of your decency by force. Guard *that* at *all* costs.

5

"Here am I. Send me." Let these words from scripture be your answer when the call comes for someone to stand against the forces of evil, corruption, and decadence. Do not presume that you will emerge from the conflict unscathed. Indeed, do not presume that you will emerge at all. That is none of your concern. Yours is to heed the call of duty even if the cause appears utterly lost, and the hope of victory has receded to the point of vanishing. What is all this talk of victory and defeat to you? Is the matter entirely in your hands? It is not. Your conduct should be your only concern. What is the noble path? Find it. Do not depart from it. It leads where you wish to go.

6

There is frequently no viable alternative to patience. Often force is of no avail. Sometimes coercion is counterproductive. You will not make anyone more competent or more efficient by strangling them or breaking their bones. In many cases, the mere threat of force proves to be contrary to your goals. It is either resented, met with resistance, or it produces fear and anxiety that impede accomplishment of the intended result. Patience *can* be overextended, and it *can* be abused, or used as an excuse for lethargy, but at least as often as not, it is the only approach that holds out any promise. Learn to discern those occasions when patience is the wisest frame of mind, and develop your capacity for sustaining it. This, of course, takes patience.

7

The corrupt nearly always get their way. You have no excuse for being surprised by this—yet again! Do not tell yourself that this happens *in spite* of the will of the masses. In a democracy, the public gets what its vote determines, either directly or indirectly. The majority has no business crying "foul!" when their elected representatives do precisely the kind of things that any rational adult could have predicted. Although you have been seldom, if ever, a member of the majority, you also claim that you try to be rational, and you know that you should have seen this coming. Do not react as if you have been doused with a bucket of cold water. You steep in this world every day.

8

Your nation, your culture, and your world, *swarm* with every kind of person you can possibly imagine, and the brutally honest truth of the matter is that you want nothing to do with most of them. Perhaps this is some kind of failing on your part, but that is not *obviously* so. Do not dismiss the possibility that humankind suffers from a trans-contextual corruption, and that many of them are simply bound to be depraved—irrespective of circumstance, inclination, or opportunity. Consider the possibility that there is something irreducibly debauched and dissolute at the heart of all humanity. This includes *you*, by the way. Perhaps "we" are not the object of the creation. Perhaps we are an unintended byproduct.

9

If you are honest with yourself, you must admit that insanity is not nearly as distant from your character as you would like to believe. You can remind yourself incessantly of the methodologies of maintaining serenity, and reestablishing mental clarity, but all of these efforts also reinforce your suspicion that you are regularly in need of "booster shots" in this arena. Perhaps most people do not pay quite so much attention to the practice of self-governance, because they are either in less need of those exercises, or because they are less interested in the goal of self-mastery. If ignorance *is* bliss, then you are obligated to shun bliss. Virtue is worth the trouble. You had better *hope* it is, anyway.

10

Think of some thing or some condition that you covet, or some urge that you seek to satisfy. Now, *stop* wanting it. Renounce *all* desire pertaining to the matter. The item in question is clearly not *necessary* for your survival, as you do not currently possess the thing, nor is the condition currently satisfied—yet, here you are. You have adequate air, food, water, and shelter. In fact, you have far, *far* more than you need. Wanting what you do not have is intrinsically dissatisfying, is it not? Rather than burning your limited energies desperately grasping after this or that unnecessary augmentation to the current state of affairs, exert just a little effort of the will to repudiate interest in everything that you do not need. Why burn yourself up chasing objects of desire, when you can simply dispel the desire and be done with the chasing once and for all?

Book XXV

1

Your nation failed today. The disordered national character is, to all appearances, beyond treatment, and beyond reasonable hope of recovery. The citizens themselves are the root source of the malady. You do not live in a nation of honorable people. Perhaps you never did. You have certainly suspected as much long before today. The nation's "power brokers" (power over *what*?) have always been corrupt, shortsighted, and treacherous. They have also always been elected as representatives of the public at large. You must resist the temptation to resign to disgust and despair, but do not lie to yourself about the strength and persistence of that temptation. Of course, you can do nothing about the culture or the denizens thereof. You can do nothing about the arc of history, or your position as an insignificant speck upon it. Bear the collapse like a stalwart, if you can. If you cannot, then you have the culture that *you deserve*.

2

Secession is always an option, and not just for nations, states, or collectives. You have the power to withdraw your consent to remain voluntarily subject to the prevailing authorities. Though many may possess the *power* to detain, sanction, imprison, or expel you from civil society, *none* possess the legitimate *moral authority* to subjugate you or your will. It is within your direct power to secede, as a sovereign individual human being, from *any* association that you deem to be corrupt, unjust, or ignoble. No human beings, or collections thereof, are entitled to compel your allegiance, your compliance, or your respect. You may, as it were, turn away from this increasingly filthy culture and the reprobates who dominate it. First, be sure that you are not composed of the same degenerate character as they are. How certain are you concerning this last issue? Was that a slight chill up your spine just now? There is, after all, a degenerate in nearly every mirror.

3

Detach yourself emotionally and psychologically from the news of the day. Do not *ignore* it. Do not attempt to pretend it away, or imagine brighter possibilities than the available evidence can support. An escapist delusion is not a solution to any problem, and it is no proper part of any plan to address future contingencies. You *must* pay attention, but you must *not* allow your peace of mind to depend upon events magically conforming to your wishful thinking or your stubbornly held expectations. In fact, hope is always misplaced when it is vested in the vicissitudes of the political, social, or economic spheres. Your hopes are to be attached *only* to your own efforts of will, and your own diligent attention to self-discipline. You must *hope* that *you* have the fortitude to meet the challenges that you encounter. Captain your own ship, and chart a course toward wisdom and virtue. Do not, however, insist upon commanding the sea.

4

Empathy is a valuable inclination of character and well worth cultivating. It affords insight into the causes and consequences of our psychological tendencies and behavioral inclinations. Accurately predicting general responses to events is useful in dealing with friend and foe alike. It is also indispensable for determining the likelihood of future occurrences of significant social scale. You cannot have much of an idea of how people are going to behave unless you have a reasonably judicious understanding of their motivations, desires, and aversions. Your purpose is not to govern, or even to influence, anyone to behave this way or that. Your purpose is to prepare for contingencies arising from events that you perceive on the horizon. You need to understand what drives most people to behave as they do. Understand others without becoming what you behold. When the time is right, do what you must. Do not hesitate due to sentimentality or empathy.

5

Justice without mercy or forgiveness makes for a hard heart and tends to inculcate cruelty of spirit. Justice with an *excess* of mercy or forgiveness tends to foster lawlessness and contempt for civility and rational governance. You do not control any system of legal justice, and you have seen the various systems in place going wrong insofar as concerns leaning toward either an excess or a deficiency of mercy and forgiveness. Neither too much nor too little of either is appropriate for you, and for your conduct concerning enactments of justice, fairness, punishment, leniency, and the like. The limited sphere in which you are enjoined to embody justice must be wisely calibrated to the offense, the offender, and any mitigating or aggravating circumstances. Judge *wisely* when you *must* judge. Remember that you must judge *your* conduct as well. Do not overflow with excessive forgiveness of your *own* misconduct.

6

By what reason are you entitled to complain of any form of (alleged) mistreatment? Do you assess your self-worth or your dignity by reference to the manner in which you are treated by others? If so, you set yourself up for needless distress and pointless indignation. You and your interests are not properly left subjected to fortuitous, unreliable circumstances such as another person's conduct, attitude, or commitment to justice. If you complain that you have been ill-used, you simply expose your own susceptibility to venality, and your deficient self-discipline. Can vice be imposed upon you by anyone apart from yourself? Can your decency be stripped from you by the hand of another, or by some passing remark about your character? Do not complain about such nonsense. These are words and deeds over which you have no control. Be a person of moral and intellectual substance. The rest is noise, wind, and trivial chatter.

7

There are aches and pains again today. You did not sleep especially well. Breakfast was not particularly satisfying. Your train of thought has been repeatedly disrupted by ambient noise, and by periodic prattle. A scheduled event did not come to fruition. Your expectations will be unmet. Are these the problems of which you complain to yourself in the confines of your unruly consciousness? What kind of pathetic weakling perseverates on such matters, and whines that these challenges are intolerable? Take a moment to compare these insignificant elements of your condition with the types of genuinely debilitating obstacles with which others have managed to cope, and in the face of which some have managed to thrive. Beethoven was all but deaf, yet he composed symphonies the likes of which the world has known neither before him nor since. How dare you whimper internally about a poor night's sleep or some piddling muscle spasm? Do not countenance this weakness in your resolve. What you tolerate tends, over time, to ossify and, gradually, it becomes part of your character.

8

What kind of blithering dolt persists in a habit that he knows to be unhealthy, unwise, and deleterious to everything that he (*claims* he) values? Is such a person not either a weakling or a charlatan who does not truly prize the things he supposedly holds dear? Does this description not apply to you? How many bad habits have you yet to expunge, though you know that they do you no good, and that they undermine your efforts to improve yourself? You simply have no excuse other than weakness or duplicitousness. Either you are lying to yourself about the centrality of self-mastery in your daily exercises, or you lack the fortitude to do what is necessary to advance that alleged interest. You tell yourself that you are appalled by your failures, yet you persist in failure. Is this the behavior of a rational being, or a mendacious fraud? Do not claim to be something that is belied by your actions.

9

The natural world cuts both ways, does it not? It explodes with beauty, majesty, subtlety, and spaces of serenity not to be found readily within any human creation. On the other hand, nature is constantly in the process of killing everything that can die, torturing everything that can suffer, and hurtling toward a state of maximal entropy, heat death, and complete dispersal and extinction of everything that has ever been valued by anyone. All natural things pass away. Beauty is transient. Life is ephemeral. Meaning dissipates and is consumed by time and space. Yet, here you are. Not for long, this life and your tiny part in the cosmos, but the *length* of your life is hardly the point. In one sense or another, the world *made* you, or some portion of the world *became* you. What a shame it would be to waste this opportunity. Determine what is *not* a waste of it. Get about *that* business right away.

10

The law is not particularly effective as a deterrent regarding illicit behavior. Surely, some would-be malefactors are forestalled by the threat of sanction or public disapprobation, but it is even more certain that punishable behavior still occurs in abundance, and vile, though not illegal, behavior occurs at least as often. If you were subject to legal sanction for every discreditable act you performed, would this not be a jailhouse journal entry? You could gripe incessantly from behind the bars. The ultimate effect might be about the same as in the actual world. What is to be made of the pervasiveness of utterly repugnant deeds, speech acts, and intentions? Is it appropriate to conclude that humanity is, in general, rotten to its core, or are your assessments of revolting comportment unfair or contrary to reasonable expectations? How much hypocrisy is entailed by your every thought on these subjects? Perhaps you indict yourself every time you look askance at human inclination. You *are* what you behold, are you not?

Book XXVI

1

Watching the corrupt avoid consequences, watching them regularly and routinely rewarded for their lies and fraudulent behavior, this has always been psychologically and emotionally challenging for you. The bile within you rises from your gut and seems to pervade your entire body. Your brain appears not to be immune from the influence of this ubiquitous bile of yours. This response is neither unnatural nor is it among the worst imaginable vices. It is, however, irrational and detrimental to your central purpose. The principle around which you allegedly organize your mental life is not well served by this tendency. It is unwise to allow an impulse or involuntary visceral response to take hold and drive your behavior or your train of thought. Indeed, you are obligated to suppress and ultimately expurgate this reflexive revulsion. Think with your brain, not with your spleen.

2

The desire for redemption is indicative of weakness and dependence. This is not an indictment of those seeking redemption—it is merely recognition that nearly everyone is weak and dependent. In fact, those who sincerely seek redemption have, at least, the advantage of realizing that they are in need of improvement, that they are flawed, and that they cannot ignore their deficiencies and still lead an honorable life. This is the same type of virtue displayed repeatedly throughout the life and relentless self-examination exhibited by Socrates. There has, arguably, never been a more reflective, self-critical human being to stride the face of the planet. The emulation of Socrates is, in most human endeavor, an ennobling adornment. Still—even Socrates was human. Had you actually met the man, you might assess his character quite differently. You will, of course, never know. The mythology is sufficient guidance in any event.

3

Something draws ever nearer. You are not certain exactly what it is, or when it shall arrive, but you detect signs of it all across a horizon that closes in, that constricts and darkens, that rumbles vaguely in this direction a little louder each day. It does not seem to have the character of your own mortality. That is an inevitability you have long recognized, and long since ceased to fear with any sincerity. Whatever it is that draws near, it is not properly to be feared (no external circumstance is), but it demands your notice, and it bids you to prepare—for what, you do not know. It will not be forestalled much longer. There are blackening skies, gathering clouds, and a scent of blood in the air. You find it baffling that so few seem to perceive its approach. You are no prophet, after all. What then are you to make of this? Is this a morbid strain in your character? Are most others simply loath to acknowledge this darkness at the edge of their perception? Perhaps it is a bit of both. In any case, the truth will become apparent sooner or later. By that time, of course, it may well be too late to do anything about it.

4

It is time to "get small." Retract the sphere of your most serious interests, and focus intently upon the rectification of your mind, your behavior, and your character. Do not allow your concern to extend to world events, politics, economics, or other wide-ranging social interests. Pay attention to circumstances and their evolution, but withdraw any attachment to things that lie beyond your control. A collapse has begun, and you do not know how precipitous or calamitous it will be. Perhaps something will emerge from the wreckage. Perhaps the wasteland awaits. You cannot know. Control the supply of necessities for your family, and marshal resources wisely. This is no time for unnecessary engagements or entanglements. It is too late for collective efforts to produce any useful outcome. Cultural self-immolation is well underway. Stand away from the flames.

5

The next time you catch yourself seeking attention, take a moment to pause and reflect upon your desire to be noticed, and consider the character of those whose attention you seek. What is the good of being seen or heard on the occasion in question? Do you seek to persuade? If so, why? Is it appropriate for you to make this attempt, with this audience, concerning this particular subject matter? If so, proceed without making a nuisance or more of a display of yourself than is necessary. If not, then shut your mouth altogether. If you do *not* seek to persuade or explain, then what is it you hope to communicate? Are you merely seeking attention for its own sake? Are you a child? Are you really so dependent upon the approval of others? This does not even qualify as vanity. Grow up, and set about the real work. Stop wasting time.

6

You should conclude each day by asking yourself how you have failed and fallen short of your responsibilities since you awoke that morning. Detail the ways in which you have disappointed your family, your friends, and your colleagues, or fallen short of your professional obligations, and your duties as a rational adult. This process is difficult, and what you observe is not going to be pretty. You are not likely to feel better about yourself when you are done. That is not, after all, the point of the exercise. Criticism is seldom a pleasant matter, and criticism of oneself *by* oneself is often the most challenging such undertaking. Rare is the person whose self-criticism is entirely trustworthy. Do not conceal your many flaws from yourself, and do not shrink from addressing your weaknesses with brutal honesty. You are, after all, the only one in a position to rectify your mind and your conduct. No one is going to swoop in and do this *for* you. Undertake this matter with the utmost urgency. You must be a light unto yourself. There is no other. Help is *not* on the way.

7

It seems that your words have caused needless trouble yet again. Do you need a muzzle? How many times will you fail to heed the counsel of your own reason? What excuse do you plan to conjure this time? You are either in possession of yourself, or you are no better than an unruly adolescent. Clearly, you have failed to think before you speak—yet again. Plainly, you are obligated to do your best to avoid failures of this type in the future. Do you take this obligation seriously? This is not a duty to make *fewer* stupid remarks, it is a duty to *eliminate* this type of behavior altogether. You speak far too frequently, and you are far too careless about the words that come out of your mouth. You too often disregard the context in which your remarks are made and the propriety of saying anything at all. Where is your forethought? Is it trapped beneath your ego? This impulse to talk without thinking must be severely curtailed. Do not open your mouth unless your intent is virtuous. Apart from that, shut up already.

8

You must be prepared to forgive your loved ones, even if they do not repent, do not admit fault, do not reciprocate in any way, and actively maintain a grudge concerning the conflict in question. You must be prepared to forgive all of that, and more too, if you wish to maintain harmony within the family and within those relationships that you value most highly. There are *very* few unforgiveable acts—especially among family. There are *some*, but these are quite rare. All too often, the problem involves conflating the unforgiveable with the merely human. It helps to recall an

142

instance of *your* most execrable conduct, and even your worst thoughts, before consigning a loved one to the oblivion of those who cannot even hope to be absolved within their own clan. *That* is a lonely condition.

9

When you wake up and clear your head of sleep's fog, you should enumerate some of the mistakes that you refuse to make in this new day. You have been granted another opportunity. Decide that you will not waste this unearned chance to improve yourself, and begin by renouncing the behaviors and thought patterns that have been gradually calcifying into bad habits. A habit, remember, is not an *excuse*. Never tell yourself that because you have been engaged in unwise or unhealthy behavior for a long time, it somehow follows that your character has been irrevocably altered or that you "cannot help" your transgressions. That is a disingenuous excuse, and exposes your weakness of will. If an ignoble tendency has plagued you for your entire life, that is all the *more* reason to exert a greater, more concerted effort against its reemergence. The time is *now*. The past holds you only insofar as you allow it to do so.

10

Decide, once and for all, whom you intend to be in this world, and then set doggedly about the project of becoming the person that you aspire to be. Do not relent for a moment. You are not permitted to "take a day off," or to indulge in a "moral holiday," to replenish your strength or give yourself a break from the rigors of self-rectification. The effect of such "holidays" tends to be quite the reverse of replenishment, does it not? Atrophy and lethargy set in quickly. Take careful inventory of your strengths, skills, and training. Take note also of your weaknesses, frailties, and inadequacies. Do not be surprised by the amount of time this accounting takes. Do not deceive yourself or allow yourself to be deceived by others. Ignore praise and blame from any source other than yourself, those whom you respect, and the wisdom of the ages, the sages, and the voice of intuition. Ignore passing trends, fads, and the received "wisdom" of the masses, the media, the punditry, and the "intellectual" class. Be the person that you must be if you are to respect yourself. Set your will in stone. Be the rock against which temptation shatters.

Book XXVII

1

By reference to what standard do you judge your character, your decency, your value as a human being, and the purpose of your continued existence? Does this standard originate outside of your own mind? If so, what is its legitimacy? Is it woven into the fabric of the universe? What justifies your adherence to it? What is the foundation from which it springs? Do not entrust your assessment of your self-worth, or the propriety of your thoughts and actions to the passing pronouncements of any alleged intelligentsia, or any congregation of your contemporaries. Yours is not an age in which wisdom, fortitude, and self-discipline are highly valued. Your era may well be a dark and unreliable representation of human excellence. Perhaps every age has been similar in this respect, but certain values and states of character seem to have endured throughout recorded history and across cultural vicissitudes. Look to the perennial virtues. There *is* a path to be found.

2

Make no pact with anyone for whom you do not have abiding respect. If your word is your bond, and you give your word to anyone disreputable, then you will be bound to disrepute, and ignoble deeds are sure to follow. If your word is *not* your bond, then you are disreputable yourself, and you should not drag another into your degenerate schemes. If your respect is well placed, you may give your word without reservation and pursue a mutually ennobling relationship or association. If your respect is misplaced, then you are either a fool who chooses to consort with untrustworthy company, or you are untrustworthy yourself, and you simply choose birds of your own feather. Carefully consider where you place your confidence—and *why*. Your associations are a reflection of your character. Whom do you see around you? You will find yourself looking back.

3

If, in the course of a debate, you feel compelled or tempted to lie, to disregard evidence, or to resort to fallacious reasoning, you must consider the possibility that you are defending an indefensible position. Either that, or your preparation and understanding of the issue in question are inadequate to the task of defending the truth. In either case, the honorable thing is to discontinue the debate, respectfully admit that you cannot sincerely persist in good faith, and withdraw with a chastened spirit. Do not further abase yourself in a dishonest or recalcitrant refusal to concede and leave your opponent in the superior position—for the time being. Sometimes, the most edifying debate is the one you lose to a wiser or more knowledgeable interlocutor. This is an opportunity to enhance your understanding, or to recognize a flaw in your worldview. Learn from your failures, or you are virtually assured of persisting in ignorance.

4

So, what is the gripe *de jour*? Some corrupt politician is not being held to account? If this surprises you, go soak your naïve head. The powerful and corrupt have always been among us and, to all appearances, will remain with us as long as there are people and power. Some colleague is dishonest, lazy, or causing you to bear the burden of extra work? So, bear it. Try to do so without whining and making a spectacle of yourself. You have worked among lazy, dishonest people your entire life. If you are obligated to report or reveal the matter, do so—but do *not* do so merely because you are put out and hope to shame the malefactor. Running to a third party to handle an interpersonal squabble of this type is neither noble nor admirable. A tattletale is hardly a figure to whom much esteem is due. Get to work on *your* capacity to manage these contingencies without losing your composure. The rest is finger pointing that you should have left behind on some playground many years ago.

5

Are you afraid? Do you fear illness? This is irrational. Do what you can to control your diet, exercise, and hygiene (both physical and psychological). Beyond this, you have little or no control over the condition of your body. A virus, bacterium, or congenital defect could lay you low at any moment. Shall you live in constant fear of conditions about which you can do nothing? What a ludicrous waste of time and energy! If that is the best that you can do, then crawl into bed, pull the covers up over your eyes, and tremble yourself to sleep. Perhaps someone will be kind enough to sing you a lullaby. Do you, on the other hand, fear the future and its contingencies? If so, there seems a simple solution, does there not? Either take that way out, or face the future like an adult, with reason and fortitude. Shake off your dread and get to work. Do not waste your life in pointless worry and anxiety. Do not become a bleeding ulcer.

6

Where, if anywhere, do you place your faith? Surely, it does not reside in other people. They have let you down, and let themselves down, far too often to be taken seriously as objects of confidence or reverence. If you are honest, you must admit that you have also let yourself down, and let others down more times than you can remember. The human mind, heart, and body are disturbingly fragile, are they not? Do you have faith that future generations of human beings will build a world superior to the one you see around you now, or that they will be superior persons to those you encounter today? Certainly not. Human character has not improved over the ages. Where is today's

Socrates, Buddha, Diogenes, or Jesus? Where is the contemporary Epictetus, or the modern day Seneca? Perhaps faith can only be placed wisely in something that does not degenerate, does not rot, and does not disintegrate over time. If you find the immutable, consider placing your faith *there*. Do not expect anyone to understand this object of your reverence should you find it. Expect ridicule instead.

7

When you fall ill, keep the matter to yourself as much and as long as is both reasonable and fitting. Do not seek sympathy or use your malady as an excuse for avoiding work or other responsibilities. It is not appropriate to talk about your suffering or your symptoms unless a physician needs this information for a diagnosis. It may be true that "misery loves company," and it is certainly true that miserly loves pity, but you are not to allow your misery to dictate your behavior or your attitude. It is well within your power to remain cheerful and rational while you contend with a virus, an injury, or some other source of discomfort. The condition of your body need not determine the condition of your consciousness. Do not break. The illness shall either kill you or you will kill it. Time will tell. In any event, neither you nor it are long for this world. Do not become hysterical about something that everyone must face.

8

If God exists, who, if anyone, has come closest to the truth about God's nature, commands, and interactions (or lack thereof) with our world? The Jews claim a national revelation at Mount Sinai. Approximately three million Israelites heard the Lord's voice. Can such an event be faked, fabricated, or otherwise invented out of whole cloth? Perhaps it is mere legend, later embraced by credulous Hebrews. Then again, perhaps it happened as described in the *Torah*. What of the Christians? Can you accept the literal resurrection of the dead? Can water transform to wine? Can someone else die and, in doing so, absolve you of *your* sins? How so? Are the Muslims correct about the alleged corruption of earlier scriptures? Is their text the inerrant recitation of Allah, through an angel, given voice by the Prophet? Should you add, "Peace be upon him"? Is the entire story a mere human invention born of ignorance, fear, delusion, or some sinister set of motives? You cannot claim to know for certain. In any event, there persists, for you, a sense of something other than the material world of matter and energy. An illusion, perhaps—but a pervasive and seemingly incorrigible one. This is at least a little odd. Of course, there is nothing unprecedented about mass delusion. Something about this itches at the back of your mind.

9

There are no second chances. There are, at most, occasional opportunities to accomplish something similar to the initial attainment that did not come to fruition. If you fail an exam once, that specific event never comes again. You may pass the same exam on a second or third try, or you may pass a similar exam, but you will do so on a different occasion under different circumstances. Just as Heraclitus pointed out that one cannot step twice into the same river, because the water flows on and is replaced by the deluge coming after, similarly, one cannot have the same experience twice, because time, matter, energy, and *oneself*, have all changed by the second attempt to do the "same" thing. You cannot try anything *again*. You can only exert yourself *anew*. Now, go forth and exert yourself anew. The alternative is stagnation— while the world swirls around you and time flows ever onward.

10

You perceive instability in nearly every direction. A military coup in Turkey (was it not once "Asia Minor"?) this week. As it turns out, a *failed* coup. Terrorist attacks have become such a commonplace that they now elicit groans rather than gasps. Economies, the world over, appear to balance upon a razor's edge. The moral compass seems to shift from place to place and, in some quarters, from day to day. Many reject the very notion of good and evil. The center does not seem likely to hold. Indeed, you begin to wonder about the very concept of a "center" to all or any of it. No matter how chaotic events may seem, you must not allow yourself to loosen your grip upon the principles to which you cling, and by which your decisions and actions ought to be guided. Nothing in your experience convinces you that anything surpasses reason as a guiding light. Nothing convinces you that anything surpasses wisdom and virtue as proper objects of your attention and efforts. The pole star does not cease to exist amid the storm. Even when you cannot see it, try to follow it "by raw feel." This counsel may rest upon wishful thinking. So be it.

Book XXVIII

1

Scripture tells us that the hand wrote "TEKEL" on the King's wall, and upon learning its translation, the King began to dissolve in anguish and despair. The Aramaic term "TEKEL" means (roughly) "thou art weighed in the balances and found wanting." If this is an apt description of anyone, it certainly seems to apply to *you*. Clearly, you can only be found "wanting" by any honest standard of measure. In fact, "wanting" is one of the more charitable descriptors available. Unlike the King, however, you will not dissolve in despondency. This judgment cannot frighten you at all, as you have long ago rendered it against yourself. From the time your mind was "of the age of reason," you have been acutely aware of your deficiencies, weakness, and faults. This awareness is a call to action, a call to the assiduous practice of self-discipline, and a call to awaken. You have no kingdom to lose. Work until you perish. This is as close as you are likely to come to living a noble life.

2

Disrespectful children are indicative of poor parenting and, in many cases, the general deterioration of the surrounding culture. You cannot do much about the latter. The levers of cultural influence are not yours to manipulate. As for the parenting, this is one of your most sacred obligations. It is essential that you know your children and understand their habits of thought and behavior well enough to anticipate problems before they arise or, at the very least, before the behavioral problems become entrenched and incorrigible. Do not allow your children to become strangers to you. This is more challenging than it may, at first, appear. Though they grow up in your home, they do not grow up in the same cultural milieu as your generation experi-

151

enced (to say nothing of those generations preceding yours). Do not let them drift away from you, and from your guiding hand, before they are prepared to steer for themselves, and before they have identified the values that shall guide them.

3

Exhibitionism is a tawdry thing, is it not? A useful skill should be cultivated, but there is no good reason to make a show of your abilities, or of your supposed prowess. Is it not a mark of weakness and dependence upon external approval that makes you feel compelled to perform tricks for applause, reward, or public acclaim? You either conduct yourself in ennobling fashion, or you do not. Once ennobled, you accomplish nothing further by playing to the crowd and begging for some expression of affection. Indeed, this is *contrary* to your primary goal. You do not increase your independence of will by beseeching others for their attention or approval. A good human being need not endeavor to be *seen as* a good human being. Virtue is either its own reward, or it has none. If its value is mere utility, then you treat your character as just another commodity. Be careful about placing yourself up for sale.

4

Suppose you successfully exact revenge for some wrong, real or imagined, perpetrated against you or "yours." What virtuous aim is thereby accomplished? Have you made yourself wiser, nobler, or in any other way improved your character? Merely assuaging the impulse to inflict pain for pain, or humiliation for the sake of causing suffering like your own, is certainly nothing to celebrate. The strike-back impulse is common among many of the "lower" animals. To satisfy this urge is bestial, and answers to no rationally justifiable principle of good conduct. A cat is motivated in this way. It will seek to harm the perceived cause of its pain or discomfort. Are you no better than a cat? Are you not ashamed to live according to some animalistic creed? If you cannot rise above such urges, perhaps you belong in a kennel or on the end of a leash. If reason is to be your master, you must resist base impulses. This is neither simple nor easy. That is no excuse for surrendering to the mere brute within you.

5

It is easy to become overly impressed with degrees, titles, and mass acclaim. None of these are evidence of wisdom, virtue, or even intellectual prowess. You have known far too many imbeciles with doctoral degrees to be taken in by such trifles. You have also encountered far too many enlightened beings among the "unlearned" to discount an opinion merely because it is presented by someone wearing overalls as opposed to a suit jacket with patches on the elbows. Indeed, are not the "intellectuals" of your era far more culpable for the cultural decay that you perceive than are all of the mechanics, plumbers, electricians, and construction workers put together? If the youth are being corrupted, it is hardly the fault of the carpenters and the trash collectors. Who produces the films, music, academic gibberish, and other symptoms of cultural pathology that infect your era? No janitor ever convinced the masses to abase themselves.

6

Once the die is cast, do not waste time considering counterfactual consequences or imaginary antecedents. The way that a thing "might have been" is of little use when contemplating how to respond to the way that the thing actually *is*. Your responsibilities lie in dealing with the world as it stands, and you do not satisfy these responsibilities by allowing yourself to become consumed with regret, or fantasy about possibilities not realized. Look at the tangible events in which you find yourself enmeshed. Reason about your genuine condition. Consider the possible responses to the real challenges with which you are presented. In light of all the information you can gather, make the most rational decision you can, regarding the proper behavior of a virtuous, honorable person. Manifest that decision in action. Do not allow yourself to look back with regret. This is an essential element of the formula for building a noble character.

7

You are a human being, but you *are* an animal as well. You are a primate, you are a mammal, and you are just one of untold billions to have walked, crawled or slithered upon the face of this planet. Do not disregard millions of years of evolutionary imperatives, or the kinship with other living things implied in shared genetics, environment, and biological and neurological homologies. Do not require or expect a level of intellectual or rational attainment that is precluded by the bestial inheritance with which you, and your fellow human beings, are endowed. Also, do not turn up your nose at the beast within you. The instincts, the reflexes, and the impulses deriving from the limbic system are crucial for survival, and essential for understanding those around you, and anticipating their interests and behavior. You live among talking apes, and it is unwise to pretend that you walk among the angels.

8

How often you recur to sluggishness each day! Can you not sustain an effort beyond the first few steps of a process or procedure? Far too often, you allow yourself to be distracted by utterly insignificant nonsense. It is almost as if you are looking for an excuse to shove aside your assigned duties in order to pursue some tangent, or some inessential flight of fancy. Do not tell yourself that this is "normal," or make up fairy tales about limitations on your attention span. Like any other form of endurance, enhancing your attention takes work, discipline, and diligent training. Are you like a small child who chases butterflies when there are chores to be done? If a task does not sustain your attention of its own accord, make note of your wandering mind, chastise yourself quickly and efficiently, and get back to the business at hand. Do not complain of boredom. Rouse your interest like an adult with a job to do.

9

You have occasion to experience contempt for other people— almost certainly more often than is healthy. In most cases, this attitude is both unwise and unwarranted. Consider how much *more* frequently you experience contempt for yourself, and for your many flaws. Is this attitude equally unwise and unwarranted? If so, you clearly overindulge to your own detriment. If not, what is it about you that warrants excess disdain? Can it be that your contempt attaches to the human condition in general, or to the all too common maladies and dysfunctions to which it is susceptible? That might explain why your scorn alights upon your own character more often than those of all others put together. You have far more frequent experience of your own pathologies, stupidities, and weaknesses, than you do with the similar faults of others. Perhaps you are getting a bit sick and tired of yourself. Is this really so surprising? You have spent your entire life irritating yourself with your whining, whimpering, petty anxieties, and incessant busy-bodying. Can you not leave yourself alone for a moment?

10

More often than you would like to admit, you wake with a clouded mind, and you struggle with forgetfulness early in the day. Is this a symptom of some eventual full-blown senility or dementia? Is this an indication of unwise and unhealthy habits coming home to roost? Is it a more common phenomenon than you realize and, if so, does that make it any less a legitimate object of your notice? If there is something that you can do about this type of malfunction, then you must do what is necessary. A reasonably well-performing mind is about all you have ever had to offer anyone. Is there some other argument in favor of your continued existence? If your mind goes, you will be a burden to your family, useless to yourself, and bereft of the only one of nature's gifts that set you apart from the other apes. You have no business outliving your usefulness. A life can be wasted in the sense that one lives too long, or lives without purpose, just as a life can be wasted in the sense that one dies before having a chance to discover one's purpose. Do not stay longer than you can justify. Show yourself out before you allow yourself to decline to the level of a sentient vegetable.

Book XXIX

1

Honesty requires practice and discipline, as does any other form of performance art. At first, telling uncomfortable truths is no easy matter. You must begin with basics. Much as you begin to discipline your body with simple exercises like push-ups, sit-ups, basic squats, and light running, similarly, you begin developing your honesty and fortitude by telling simple truths about quotidian matters. Be honest when describing the events of your day. Have you accomplished very little by lunchtime? Say so. Do not pretend to have worked harder or done more than the facts and evidence will bear. Did you enjoy your day, or did you become bored or disenchanted with something, perhaps yourself, somewhere along the way? Describe your experience as it happened. Do not embellish, and do not leave out any embarrassing details. Have you failed to be sufficiently grateful for the unearned opportunities of a new day? Admit it. Say it out loud. Gradually, you can become honest about your greatest flaws, your most mortifying peccadilloes, and those facets of your character about which you are most ashamed. *That* will be real progress.

2

Whom did you seek to impress today, and for what purpose did you wish to be impressive? If you seek anything other than virtue, wisdom, and the improvement of the deficient areas of your character, count the day as a loss and yet another exercise in failure and degradation. Do you carry yourself with an eye to others who might be observing you? Do you speak (or write) with the intention of displaying your alleged intellectual and semantic prowess, rather than with the purpose of communicating clearly and effectively? If so, why are you not walking around holding out a tin cup? Why not just straightforwardly beg alms from strangers? Perhaps a leash is the proper accessory for you after all. Either conduct yourself like an adult who aims at wise self-governance, or admit that you are the equivalent of an emotional panhandler. Go ahead and humiliate yourself before your family, friends, colleagues, and passing strangers. Tell them that you are incapable of persisting without their approval. Does the prospect not appeal to you? Does it seem base and unworthy of an autonomous adult? Perhaps there is hope after all.

3

Games of chance and games of skill are separated by far less than you might like to imagine. What, in the final analysis, distinguishes luck from skill? Does the latter depend upon one's performance and one's acquired abilities? Certainly. How does one manage to acquire skills, abilities, and various forms of expertise? Does luck not lie at the root of all such acquisition? Is it not good fortune that permits mental and motor skills to combine in such a fashion as to provide an advantage? If it is not, at root, luck, then what explains elevated ability or understanding? Intrinsic qualities do not arise because you earned them. Base level abilities arise because of heredity and environment. Did you secure your genetic inheritance by force of will? Did you fix circumstances surrounding your birth by fiat or by dint of expertise? Give thanks for your good fortune and move forward. Do not complain of the many admirable qualities that you lack, and do not boast of any virtues that you may imagine you possess. The cards were dealt long ago. Play them.

4

Everyone is beset by difficulties, challenges, and problems on all sides. These can, mostly, be addressed in a better or worse fashion. All can, in principle, be rectified—except, of course, the insistence that one *must not be* best by difficulties, challenges, and problems. If you wish to be free of all encumbrances, by all means, put an end to yourself and your whining as soon as the opportunity arises. To live in this world, as a human being, is to live in the presence of suffering, discontent, and pervasive dissatisfaction. If doing so is "beneath you," or "too much for you," then, by all means, go and find the nearest exit. At every turn, a door leads out and away from this "vale of tears." Quit your crying. Go! Either step through one of those doors, or rouse your courage and stop behaving like a malignant tumor upon the body of humankind. Grow up or get shut of the world once and for all.

5

Who imagines counterfactual possibilities without some degree of self-aggrandizement? Surely, *some* do, but do *you*? Even when you fantasize about hermitage or life as an abject failure, a transient, an addict, or muse about an early death, you always tinge such circumstances with notes of nobility. What is so noble about you here and now that you imagine its persistence across all of these possible realities? What have you accomplished that is worth holding up to the world with pride? Has anyone ever wanted to be like you, to emulate your conduct or your character? If so, no one has made a show of it. If not, it is probably worth asking yourself why no one has chosen you as an exemplar. The answer is fairly obvious, is it not? You are not worthy of anyone's admiration. How are you similar to Socrates, Buddha, Jesus, Diogenes, Alexander the Great, or any other noble figure from history? You are genetically a member of the same species. The similarities end there, do they not?

6

The natural world is sufficiently beautiful that a God who fails to exist is really missing out on the view. You suspect that this not a worthwhile concern. The fundamental constants governing the cosmos appear to be finely tuned, and expertly engineered, for life—perhaps even for *human* life. Indeed, the *absence* of design would constitute something of a miracle! Why should there not be a universe, why should there not be an *infinite* ensemble of universes, entirely devoid of even the most rudimentary forms of life? Are there not an infinite variety of possible cosmological circumstances within which life does *not* evolve? You are *here* to contemplate such matters. Both meanings are intended. You either exist as part of God's divine creation, or you exist as a spontaneous, unguided concurrence of events so improbable as to constitute the probabilistic equivalent of a miracle. In either case, it is legitimate to use the term "sin" to refer to your failure to appreciate this opportunity fully, and to your penchant for grumbling about little annoyances. Where is your gratitude? Where is your sense of awe and wonder? Wake up, you fool.

7

Your accomplishments are few, unimpressive, and more than counterbalanced by your many failures, and by a river of mediocrity running through the center of your life, right up to the present moment. Your middling mind, your feeble character, and your paltry efforts, more than anything else about you, are your most salient distinguishing features. How ordinary you are! Are there more than a handful of features, abilities, or attainments in which you may justly take solace? Are there even a handful? Is there *one* to which you can point and say, with confidence and sincerity, "*That* is why my life mattered"? If you were to write out a comprehensive list of your virtues and admirable achievements, how much paper and ink would you need? Can you not read through these very pages and perceive the dearth of nobility, and the absence of excellence? Consider the possibility that the entire project is an embarrassing waste of time. Do not interpret "project" too narrowly.

8

In a social situation, you too frequently seek either attention or an anonymous and disdainful distance from all festivities. You are disinclined to moderation in these matters. Perhaps you are disinclined to life altogether. If you cannot be the center of attention, you tend to retreat into relative isolation, and lose interest in the available interpersonal interactions. It is as if you fancy yourself something special, something worthy of particular interest, and you peevishly withdraw if the others on hand regard you as nothing of importance. Surely, you cannot believe that you are *entitled* to approval, attention, or respect. Consider how ridiculous you would judge anyone else asserting such a claim. Whom do you believe yourself to be? How do you think you are generally regarded? What commends you as a fit object of anyone's attention on any occasion? Do not put on airs as if you deserve some pride of place. Accept the fact that you are no one special, you will live your whole life and die as no one special, and after you are gone, know that your entire life will be forgotten. This is as it should be. Of what other lives have you taken note? How does your life, how do your accomplishments, compare to those? Your delusions of grandeur are idiocy heaped upon mediocrity.

9

What is keeping you awake at night? It cannot be any form of material need. Most of the human race has never had access to the comforts that you take for granted. Looking around you, it is clear that you want for nothing—yet, you manage to feel ill at ease somehow. Perhaps you are subject to some biochemical "imbalance" or abnormality that renders you especially susceptible to anxiety and distress. If so, what do you intend to do about it? The condition is not likely to be remedied by one discreet exertion of will. The problem may well be *inside* of you. Your brain may be defective. Thus, if your condition proves to be innate or congenital (though you do not *know* this to be the case), your only option is to endure, assiduously increase your tolerance of this form of discomfort and, gradually, improve your resistance to the ill effects of this disordered neuro-chemical condition. Expect this process to be long, arduous, and potentially frustrating—but do not become dispirited. With reasonable expectations and goals clear before your mind, move forward and face whatever challenges may arise. Endure, persevere, and you may emerge stronger for your efforts. This may be the best outcome for which it is sensible to hope.

10

You failed again yesterday. Is there a single day of your life that you have lived entirely in accordance with the principles and values that you espouse, both publicly and within the confines of your own consciousness? When was the last time you practiced what you preached for more than a few moments? Your hypocrisy is deep and abiding, is it not? Without adherence to maxims founded in reason, virtue, and sincerity, you know that your life will devolve into wretchedness and ignominy. You have seen the unprincipled life up close. You have watched the wake of destruction it leaves both within and without. You have beheld the malformations of character, the moral disfigurement, and the self-abasement that ensue when decency is jettisoned, or subordinated to licentious self-indulgence. Do you fear any condition more than dishonor, dissolution, and degeneracy? No one could tell as much by observing your behavior. These fates all await you should you stray far or long from the proper path. Perhaps your greatest fear is that you are not up to the rigors of the righteous life. Perhaps this fear is well warranted. Do you *know* that this course is *not* too difficult for you? There is, it seems, only one way to find out. Get moving.

Book XXX

1

If the future appears dark, embrace the darkness. Come to know it, understand it, and internalize the darkness as much as is necessary to respond to events as they arise. The alternative is disingenuous self-deception, or willful ignorance. Neither you nor anyone else will benefit from fantasizing about a future that is clearly not to be. Some say that it is wise to hope for the best, but prepare for the worst. You are, hopefully, honest enough to admit that the first step is a waste of time. Hope never forestalls a hopeless future. If it is on its way, hope will not stand athwart any event that approaches. Hope is for children, and for those that embrace pleasant delusion, rather than realistic acceptance of actual events, and the inevitable consequences of one's engagement with them. Hopes realized are always based upon a rational evaluation of the available evidence, and a careful assessment of probabilities. Reasonable inferences may then be drawn. Hopes dashed are not, in fact, properly called "hopes" at all. They are manifestations of a stubborn refusal to see what one does not wish to see.

2

Everything that *can* suffer, *does* suffer. Everything that *can* die, *will* die. You have suffered, you will suffer much more, and a lifetime of your suffering will culminate in your death. When you can muster genuine gratitude for all of *that*, then you will have made the kind of progress that is not easily reversed. To develop sincere appreciation for this opportunity to be born in a brutal world, not of your making, to struggle and fail time and time again, to feel repeatedly lost, bewildered, frustrated, and hopeless, to swim in this ocean of misery, and, ultimately, to drown in it—this is the beginning of wisdom. You must embody overwhelming gratitude for the opportunity to fail repeatedly, with no guarantee of eventual success, and to wade cheerfully into a doomed struggle against time and your own limitations. You clamber toward your own death across a landscape of thorns, broken glass, and the corpses of those who have gone before you. Would you have it any other way?

3

No one ever *owes* you an explanation, an apology, or a helping hand. Insistence to the contrary is juvenile, and it sets you up to become disappointed and resentful when your expectations are unsatisfied. You are obligated to do what you believe to be the right thing at *all* times, irrespective of any expectation of reward, acknowledgement, or expressions of gratitude. How many times, after all, have you failed to appreciate undeserved benefits you have derived from the labor and exertions of persons you do not even know, and that you have never even heard of? Have you expressed gratitude, even in the privacy of your own mind, for the many advances in agriculture, engineering, medicine, or other areas of applied technology, without which your life would be immeasurably more difficult? Only a small-minded hypocrite demands obeisance from family, friends, and associates, while failing to take note of all the benefits received from both the ages, and from unsung contemporaries. As for apologies, you may demand them only after you have issued them to *everyone* you have ever wronged. Have you got a lifetime to spare?

4

Stand-up comics might be the only people who can still tell the truth these days without risking the disapprobation of their peers, ostracism, and perhaps even their careers. In fact, even some comedians have, of late, complained about the constraints of political correctness, and the avid enforcement of the "speech police," who seek to rouse the masses against anyone who deviates from the permitted forms of expression. This authoritarian crackdown on formerly free speech is troubling, insofar as it infringes upon the liberties of those who submit to threats and intimidation tactics, but it need not hamper *you* in any way whatsoever. Are you incapable of forming "forbidden" sounds with your mouth, or contemplating proscribed thoughts and theories within the confines of your own mind? The speech acts may incur penalties, to be sure, but who guaranteed you that speaking your mind would entail no consequences? Do not grouse about your Constitutional Rights or their curtailment. If you need a document to affirm your control over your tongue and voice box, then you probably have no thoughts worthy of anyone's attention in any case. Speak the truth. Let the chips fall where they may. What do you care for "chips"?

5

You had that recurring dream again last night. It is not exactly the same dream, but every instance is of a general type. There is something crucial that you absolutely *must* accomplish, or horrible consequences will befall your family, or your nation, or the world at large. Sometimes, the fate of all humanity hangs in the balance. Your goal is clear, your plan is viable, your success seems all but assured — and, every time, some trivial obstruction prevents you from making any progress. You are stuck at "square one," squabbling with some bureaucrat, or struggling to surmount a wall that popped up out of nowhere, or repeatedly explaining the urgency of your situation to some dull-witted security guard who insists that you produce "the password," or perform some pointless ritual. This is your frustration dream. The thing that you find troubling, and the problem for which you cannot help but blame yourself, is that everything in your dream is a manifestation of *your* unconscious. *You* are inventing these annoying hindrances, and *you* become increasingly exasperated by them. You cannot seem to get out of *your own* way. Surely, this reveals something about your waking life as well. The greatest impediment to your success is *you*. This is nearly always the explanation for your many failures, is it not? You are either unwilling, or unable, to simply get out of your own way. Perhaps the idea of genuine progress frightens you. Either overcome this self-sabotage, or get comfortable with failure.

6

Disturbingly many claims that you regard as both obviously false, and broadly toxic to your culture, have become not merely commonplace presumptions, but have actually ascended to the condition of unchallengeable orthodoxy. Dissent seems to be prohibited, and dissidence incurs penalties that most dare not confront. The "Ignoble Lie" has become standard messaging in education, in the media, among politicians, and several genera-tions have, by now, been weaned on a passel of lies, and immersed in a worldview that bears almost no resemblance to reality—or so it seems to you. You know that repeating a lie often enough does *not*, contrary to the popular saying, cause it to become the truth. You also know, however, that repeating a lie often enough can cause it to be embraced, and acted upon, *as if it were* the truth. *That* is the real cause for pessimism concerning the present and future generations who will steep in falsehood without ever realizing that they have done so. It is your duty to expose this campaign of disinformation, and to supplant this false narrative with the truth, insofar as you are able. Do not expect to persuade the masses. Do not insist upon overturning the prevailing falsehoods, and establishing a new culture of honesty. This is not within your control. You *must*, however, speak out against this insidious cultural hypnosis. If you are not prepared to defend the truth against all comers, and irrespective of any consequence, you are not what you claim that you strive to be. Is your entire adulthood a mere pretense? If so, why trouble yourself about lies taken for truth? What are you becoming?

7

He might have been able to endure his suffering with fortitude and grace, if the Bible's Job had only been presented with some justification for its warrant. You will find that you can persevere through just about any trial, if you only have a good reason to endure. The human capacity to bear suffering is fairly impressive, but you often need some motivation beyond your own survival to help you withstand the most devastating blows that the world is capable of delivering. You can be fairly confident that the world is going to hurt you, it is going to demoralize you, it is going to rip hope away from you repeatedly, and then it is going to kill you. No one survives life in this world. You will *not* be the first. What then, you may wonder, is the point? Why put yourself through all of the trials and tribulations that seem to be ineradicable elements of the human condition, if you just drop dead when it is over? The answer is, perhaps, a little too simple. You do it because you are here, and the alternative is cowardice. Only a coward deserts his post for fear of injury and death. Do *not* abandon your post. There is either a reason that you are here, or there is not. That is not up to you. What you do, and what you make of yourself in the time you have, that is *all* that is up to you. Is the world "unfair"? So be it — and so what? Now, go forth and endure.

8

Children forge their character by modeling the behavior of the adults with whom they are most closely associated. This is why parental advice so frequently seems to fall on deaf ears. When the advice offered does not comport with the behavior that the child observes, the force of the spoken word is blunted by the greater influence of the evident character of the hypocrite offering the advice. Instructing a child to, "Do as I say, and not as I do," has always been relatively fruitless. Just as ducklings imprint and exhibit the behavior of the duck, so too do children absorb and display the character of the parent, and of other role models they may encounter. For this reason, as well as others intrinsic to your attempts to be a decent human being, you are obligated to *be* as virtuous as you are able, and you are not permitted to rest content with verbal admonitions about virtue and vice. It is not enough to "talk a good game" to young people. They tend to "see more clearly than they hear" so to speak. An ersatz excellence will be uncovered as a sham. No one knowingly emulates a phony. Your virtue must be real. Your decency must be sincere. Otherwise, you are just an actor playing a false role. You have a *genuine* role to play. Get to it. Think of the children.

9

So much of the news of the day is alarming. Much of the news seems designed and intended to foster fear and exacerbate anxiety. The plan seems to be working fairly effectively. Almost everyone that you meet is prepared to speak at length about their fears, worries, and intensifying concerns. Interestingly, when pressed for details about what it is, precisely, that scares them and keeps them on edge, most of your friends and associates have little to offer beyond vague, hand-waving generalities about the "coarsening of the culture," or the "pressures of the market-place," or about "these kids today," and their various adolescent deficiencies. The angst appears to be fairly "free-floating" and nebulous. Perhaps this is precisely the intent of the powers that be. A frightened populace that does not quite know what it fears is probably more likely to turn to the powerful for protection and guidance. On the other hand, there may well be no organized effort at work in this matter at all. Perhaps the contemporary world just fosters disquiet because it really has become cold, indifferent, and confusing. You need not seek root causes regarding the matter. All you need to do is clearly identify your most fundamental guiding principles, and adhere to them, irrespective of the vicissitudes of modernity, or the bleating of the herd. Does an allegedly horrifying apparition present itself before you? Perhaps it does. True honor and genuine strength of character do not crumble or dissolve before any apparition. Smile back at the bogeyman. Wave him in, and see who shatters first.

10

Keep the first stanza of the Serenity Prayer close to your heart and easily accessible to your conscious mind:

> God grant me the serenity
> to accept the things I cannot change;
> courage to change the things I can;
> and wisdom to know the difference.

You need not believe in a literal God for the message to gain purchase with your contemplation of difficulties, challenges, and problems, or the resolve with which you face these tribulations each day. There may well be a God who takes note of your struggles, and who offers you guidance to the path and plan laid down for you. There may be no such thing, and it may be that all talk of the transcendent, the otherworldly, and the holy serves only to herd the sheep into churches, synagogues, and mosques—so that they may be fleeced more efficiently. This is not up to you. Remember that you seek serenity and virtue through the dogged pursuit of wisdom at all costs. The wisdom to become a decent and honorable human being is your ultimate goal. As for the things you cannot change, you may as well accept them. The alternative is not at all clear. What you *can* change lies within you. You can change your character and your behavior. You *can* change your way of "being in the world," and your interactions with persons and events. You only need the *courage* to pursue wisdom, and to face each new day with strength of character and fortitude. Serenity can be had. Courage is necessary. Virtue is the heart of the matter. Wisdom is the essence of all these. Go forth and pursue wisdom for all that you are worth. That is all.

BOOKS

O-BOOKS
SPIRITUALITY

O is a symbol of the world, of oneness and unity; this eye represents knowledge and insight. We publish titles on general spirituality and living a spiritual life. We aim to inform and help you on your own journey in this life. If you have enjoyed this book, why not tell other readers by posting a review on your preferred book site? Recent bestsellers from O-Books are:

Heart of Tantric Sex
Diana Richardson
Revealing Eastern secrets of deep love and intimacy to Western couples.
Paperback: 978-1-90381-637-0 ebook: 978-1-84694-637-0

Crystal Prescriptions
The A-Z guide to over 1,200 symptoms and their healing crystals
Judy Hall
The first in the popular series of five books, this handy little guide is packed as tight as a pill-bottle with crystal remedies for ailments.
Paperback: 978-1-90504-740-6 ebook: 978-1-84694-629-5

Take Me To Truth
Undoing the Ego
Nouk Sanchez, Tomas Vieira
The best-selling step-by-step book on shedding the Ego, using
the teachings of *A Course In Miracles.*
Paperback: 978-1-84694-050-7 ebook: 978-1-84694-654-7

The 7 Myths about Love...Actually!
The journey from your HEAD to the HEART of your SOUL
Mike George
Smashes all the myths about LOVE.
Paperback: 978-1-84694-288-4 ebook: 978-1-84694-682-0

The Holy Spirit's Interpretation of the New Testament
A course in Understanding and Acceptance
Regina Dawn Akers
Following on from the strength of *A Course in Miracles*, NTI
teaches us how to experience the love and oneness of God.
Paperback: 978-1-84694-085-9 ebook: 978-1-78099-083-5

The Message of A Course In Miracles
A translation of the text in plain language
Elizabeth A. Cronkhite
A translation of *A Course in Miracles* into plain, everyday
language for anyone seeking inner peace. The companion
volume, *Practicing A Course In Miracles*, offers practical lessons
and mentoring.
Paperback: 978-1-84694-319-5 ebook: 978-1-84694-642-4

Rising in Love
My Wild and Crazy Ride to Here and Now, with Amma, the
Hugging Saint
Ram Das Batchelder
Rising in Love conveys an author's extraordinary journey of
spiritual awakening with the Guru, Amma.
Paperback: 978-1-78279-687-9 ebook: 978-1-78279-686-2

Thinker's Guide to God
Peter Vardy
An introduction to key issues in the philosophy of religion.
Paperback: 978-1-90381-622-6

Your Simple Path
Find happiness in every step
Ian Tucker
A guide to helping us reconnect with what is really important in
our lives.
Paperback: 978-1-78279-349-6 ebook: 978-1-78279-348-9

365 Days of Wisdom
Daily Messages To Inspire You Through The Year
Dadi Janki
Daily messages which cool the mind, warm the heart and guide
you along your journey.
Paperback: 978-1-84694-863-3 ebook: 978-1-84694-864-0

Body of Wisdom
Women's Spiritual Power and How it Serves
Hilary Hart
Bringing together the dreams and experiences of women across
the world with today's most visionary spiritual teachers.
Paperback: 978-1-78099-696-7 ebook: 978-1-78099-695-0

Dying to Be Free
From Enforced Secrecy to Near Death to True Transformation
Hannah Robinson
After an unexpected accident and near-death experience,
Hannah Robinson found herself radically transforming her life,
while a remarkable new insight altered her relationship with
her father; a practising Catholic priest.
Paperback: 978-1-78535-254-6 ebook: 978-1-78535-255-3

The Ecology of the Soul
A Manual of Peace, Power and Personal Growth for Real People
in the Real World
Aidan Walker
Balance your own inner Ecology of the Soul to regain your
natural state of peace, power and wellbeing.
Paperback: 978-1-78279-850-7 ebook: 978-1-78279-849-1

Readers of ebooks can buy or view any of these
bestsellers by clicking on the live link in the title. Most
titles are published in paperback and as an ebook.
Paperbacks are available in traditional bookshops. Both
print and ebook formats are available online.

Find more titles and sign up to our readers' newsletter at
http://www.johnhuntpublishing.com/mind-body-spirit

Follow us on Facebook at
https://www.facebook.com/OBooks/
and Twitter at https://twitter.com/obooks